The Value Controversy in Sociology

*A New Orientation
for the Profession*

Dennis C. Foss

The Value
Controversy
in Sociology

Jossey-Bass Publishers
San Francisco • Washington • London • 1977

THE VALUE CONTROVERSY IN SOCIOLOGY
A New Orientation for the Profession
by Dennis C. Foss

Copyright © 1977 by: Jossey-Bass, Inc., Publishers
615 Montgomery Street
San Francisco, California 94111
&
Jossey-Bass Limited
28 Banner Street
London EC1Y 8QE

Library of Congress Catalogue Card Number LC 77-82915

International Standard Book Number ISBN 0-87589-348-1

Manufactured in the United States of America

JACKET DESIGN BY WILLI BAUM

FIRST EDITION

Code 7746

The Jossey-Bass
Social and Behavioral Science Series

Preface

Let me start with a confession: I am a young sociologist. In fact, I'm just starting my career. When I told many people who were well ensconced as social scientists that I intended to work in the area of values, I met considerable resistance. They were kind enough to make clear that they did not doubt my ability, but they felt that the value question is not the proper domain of a young sociologist—that while the question of what goals sociologists seek is important, it is better left to more mature scholars. I found this response puzzling and disconcerting.

I never really pressed them as to why they held this opinion. One idea seemed to be that at the end of your life you are better able to reflect on where the discipline has been and where it is going, and thus you are able to offer advice to those who follow you. Louis Coser (1969) offers this kind of advice in his "Letter to a Young Sociologist." The idea that considerable insight comes with age makes sense, and I think a young sociologist would be foolish not to consider carefully the understanding reached by those who have "been there." Another reason offered was that it would be unwise for a young sociologist to commit himself to a position in print that he might later reject. While it might be awkward, I suspect that I could survive such a recanting if it seemed warranted. Perhaps I was urged to wait because if I had an established reputation more credence would be given to my arguments. This may be true, particularly in an area such as this, where the issues are so complex and intertwined that almost any presentation can be dismissed as naive.

But for several reasons I have gone ahead and written this book despite the well-intended advice. First, the whole question of what value stance the social sciences should take fascinates me, perhaps because on this issue even the staid language of academics cannot hide strong convictions. One can see fine minds struggling with difficult issues and with each other. Second, I feel I can add something to the debate. Many of the issues need the clarification and simplification that this book tries to supply. Also, it is time for the debate to get pushed off of the starting blocks, to get beyond the question of whether social scientists should have values and start to discuss in a meaningful way the more significant questions of what our values should be, how can we justify them, and how they relate to the knowledge we seek. I try to advance the debate in this way here, but I suspect there is a more basic reason for my attempt to write this now.

As I start my career in the discipline of sociology, it is particularly important for me to grapple with the question, "What *are* we trying to do, anyway?" This is because I do not wish to look back at the end of my career and feel that I wasted my life by putting effort into an insignificant cause, or worse still, that I helped to actualize goals that I would have opposed had I given it some thought. At the least, I wish to be able to tell myself that I *did* give it some thought. I am sure that I cannot fully decide this in advance and that my understanding of what I am trying to achieve will continually change (and hopefully grow), just as the discipline's view of its goals is continually changing. In fact, I suspect that I would feel uncomfortable if either I or my discipline accepted a particular direction without question; our answer to where we are going should be continually reanalyzed and recast.

This book is written primarily in terms of sociology. This is because I am a sociologist and therefore most familiar with the debate and literature within sociology. However, the majority of issues are relevant and basic to any social science. As a result, the questions raised should be of interest to all practicing and potential social scientists. While the reader may reject the positions advanced, it is hoped that this book will at least clarify some familiar issues, raise new issues, and either challenge or extend the reader's own position.

The book's organization roughly follows the development of my thinking in this area. The earliest position that I can remember consciously taking on the value question is that of value freedom, or neutrality with respect to all but epistemic or knowledge values. This, of course, has been the dominant position in the discipline, and Chapter One attempts to present this and closely related positions in the strongest possible form.

Like other sociologists, I have come to see that a wide variety of important social values enter sociology in many ways. As a result, the value-free position does not seem very useful either descriptively or prescriptively. Chapter Two argues in this way. While it incorporates much of what has been offered to refute the value-free position, it differs from most formulations in that it argues that the employment of values is highly *probable* rather than *necessary* and attempts to separate out the parts of the knowledge process where value incorporation is most likely. Three other initially attractive positions—sociology as value full, the ultimate benefit of sociology, and the sociological relevance positions—are also found to be inadequate for guiding and justifying the decisions involved in sociology that often involve values. Therefore, if values are likely to be employed in the decision-making process, and if we wish to justify and evaluate resulting decisions and avoid hypocrisy, then sociology as a discipline, as well as individual sociologists, must choose and make explicit a decision or goal orientation. Such an orientation will simultaneously be a reference point for decision making at the numerous stages of the knowledge-gathering process and allow evaluation and justification of the resulting decisions.

At this point, one is faced with two difficult problems. On what basis can such a decision orientation be chosen? Just what orientation should we as individuals and as members of the profession adopt? The remainder of the book is an attempt to answer these crucial questions.

Chapters Three and Five examine two different bases for choosing a decision or goal orientation that conflict in several important ways. Although arguments for each are presented, no choice is made between them. Both are argued to be sufficiently reasonable to attract a large number of adherents. Also, despite their basic disagreements, each suggests and supports the proposed *optimizing orientation*.

More specifically, Chapter Three considers what might be termed the *skeptic's view*, which asserts that the validity of basic values is ultimately not factually demonstrable and thus valued ends can only be assumed. In accordance with the skeptic's view and a corollary that values gain no additional validity by virtue of the characteristics of the individuals who possess them, sociologists have no warrant for imposing their values upon the population as a whole. If the skeptic's view is accepted, the sociologist is placed in the awkward position of having to choose a high-level decision orientation while admitting that the value of the orientation is of only assumptive validity.

Chapter Four seeks to resolve this dilemma by offering as a decision orientation the *optimization of alternatives for all individuals*. Although admittedly assumptive, this orientation has as a persuasive reason for its adoption its consonance with the skeptic's view, in that it minimizes the unwarranted imposition of values on others. A basic discussion and explication of the orientation is offered; additional discussion is presented later in the book.

Returning to the bases for a decision or goal orientation choice is an examination of an alternative *evolutionary-naturalistic* position in Chapter Five, which clearly runs counter to and is critical of the skeptic's view concerning facts as a basis for this choice. This evolutionary-naturalistic position sees the justification of values as being instrumentally tied to their function in promoting human survival and evolutionary development. Thus, the basis for choosing a decision orientation is seen as biosocial knowledge and wisdom. After the evolutionary-naturalistic view is explained, it is argued that although this view is radically different from the skeptic's view, it also suggests the merit of the choice of the optimization of alternatives for all individuals as a decision or goal orientation for sociology. Again, the work does not attempt to argue for the preferability of either basis, but instead it suggests that both are worthy of consideration and both support the proposed orientation.

Besides the basic rationales already given, additional persuasive reasons for adopting the orientation are offered in Chapter Six. Further discussion of the orientation deals with special reference to alternative orientations, the relationship of the orientation to the discipline's epistemic ethic of "truth," and possible limitations and difficulties of the orientation as proposed.

Although I consider the proposed orientation to be the most reasonable and advantageous open to sociology, it is only one alternative. I presume that other competing orientations will be advanced with differing rationales. My primary hope is that the orientation and its underlying rationales are explicated with sufficient clarity to allow both its strengths and weaknesses to emerge readily in an ensuing debate.

In addition to the usual difficulties, such as untangling the issues and searching for the right words to allow simplification of issues without distorting them, one particular difficulty encountered deserves special mention. In dealing with a topic as basic to the discipline as its values, an exceedingly wide range of areas of knowledge and argument are relevant and must be referred to. Many of them necessarily fall outside the author's discipline and specialization. In short, what is often given brief consideration here would be the topic of volumes by specialists in those areas. As a result, the necessary breadth of the discussion demands what may at times seem a cursory or insufficiently qualified discussion in the eyes of the specialists. However, it is assumed that such basic and far-ranging discussions are necessary and that such inadequacies will quickly be pointed out so that this important debate can continue.

Acknowledgments

This work was made possible in part by the Center for the Study of Middle-Sized Cities of the public affairs division of Sangamon State University, and I am indebted to the Center and to Vice

President John Keiser for seeing sufficient merit in this project to provide me with partial release time for pursuing it.

Further, this work would not have been possible without the help and support of numerous individuals. Walter Buckley has personally been responsible for adding new directions to my thinking in this area and has acted as a continual stimulus for refinement and depth in the presentation. Greatly appreciated are the time, effort, and invaluable comments provided by Loren Cobb, Murray Straus, Stephen Weber, and Yutaka Yamamoto. In addition to his valuable suggestions, Straus provided the kind of confidence and support that makes a work like this possible. Yamamoto made additional contributions by clarifying some complex philosophical issues for a nonphilosopher, as well as by challenging my position in useful, insightful ways.

I am further indebted to Michael Ayers and John Munkirs for their willingness to devote much time to going over the roots of instrumentalist thinking, as well as for their persistence in carrying out what must have seemed to be endless arguments. In addition, Ayers served as a useful sounding board for new ideas as well as performed less rewarding tasks, such as tracking down unavailable source materials. Regan Smith has been highly supportive and helpful both personally and in his role as coordinator of the sociology/ anthropology program at Sangamon State University.

Howard Shapiro, Daniel Williams, Gerald Hotaling, Keith Farrington, Martha Huggins, Charles Cleveland, Charles Loos, and Harvey Bell all contributed valuable comments and conversation concerning germinal positions for the present work. Richard Dewey was not directly consulted on this work and would undoubtedly disagree with much of it, yet the clarity of his thought and his well-considered challenges to my positions have added much to the lines of thought presented.

Invaluable were the editorial and substantive suggestions made by Rich Shereikis at Sangamon State University and Anselm Strauss at the University of California, San Francisco. I am indebted to Carolyn Van Houten, Jackie Wright, Ruth Ann Ragel, and Nancy Ayers both for their willingness to struggle with the marks that I try to pass off as handwriting and their careful typing under time pressure.

From the beginning of this project, Joyce Foss has always been available to work through difficult arguments, make stylistic and editorial suggestions, react to germinal ideas, and provide much needed encouragement. Finally, if it were not for the emotional and financial support of Jean and Woody Foss, this work would not have been possible.

Springfield, Illinois   DENNIS C. FOSS
August 1977

Contents

The Author

DENNIS C. FOSS is assistant professor of sociology at Sangamon State University in Springfield, Illinois. Previously he held teaching and research assistantships, a summer fellowship, and a graduate associateship at the University of New Hampshire.

Foss received his bachelor's degree (1970) in sociology from Bates College and, concentrating in the areas of theory, social psychology, and research methods, received his master's degree (1972) and doctor's degree (1976) from the University of New Hampshire. His undergraduate honors thesis was the basis for a book, *The American View of Death: Acceptance or Denial?* (with R. G. Dumont, 1972). He has also coauthored a major review essay of theory construction and family sociology with his wife, Joyce E. Foss.

In addition to teaching, Foss's professional interests lie primarily in the philosophy of science, general systems theory, creativity, sociology of death, and the family. He enjoys interdisciplinary work and considers himself not simply a sociologist but more broadly a social scientist. At Sangamon State he is active in university governance and serves on many committees, including the University Tenure Decision Committee and the University Program Review Committee.

Foss's outside interests include the ocean, games of most types, friendly wagers, and music. He is attracted to people who get excited about what they are doing.

To Joyce Elizabeth Foss—whom I respect
as a colleague, love as a wife, and
cherish as a friend

The Value
Controversy
in Sociology

A New Orientation
for the Profession

One

Sociology:
A Value-Free Science

Sociology, like other disciplines, is faced with the basic question of what it is trying to achieve. Which goals or ends does the discipline strive for? Which ones ought it to strive for? Such questions are basic because the goals chosen, either implicitly or explicitly, influence the choices and actions of individual sociologists and set the future course of the enterprise as a whole.

When this question of orientation has been dealt with explicitly, it has been debated in terms of values or valued ends. Classic writers, such as Weber, Marx, Durkheim, and Simmel, whose works still strongly influence sociologists today, took stands on the nature of the valued ends that intellectual life should achieve. These issues were not to be faced solely by the founders of a new discipline. Although at times the issues have been more hotly debated, there has always been and continues to be strong interest in the value choices made by the discipline. The debate has evolved over time. Some "new" positions have emerged and there has been some shifting within the discipline on the issues. For example, currently there seems to be some shifting away from the predominant position of value freedom. The debate continues formally at professional meetings, in journal articles, and in letters to the editor, and more informally in classrooms, hallway conversations, and bars. But, granted the importance of the debate on sociology's goals, why does an entire volume need to be added to it, and why should someone bother to read it?

Even casual acquaintance with the debate suggests several difficulties within it which need to be addressed. First, the debate has been highly fragmented in two ways. Since issues have reared their heads in a wide variety of contexts, many context-specific issues and problems have diverted energy from the basic questions which give rise to them. Also, the debate has become fragmented due to the natural tendency to present one's own position, perhaps with some counterarguments, which makes an explicit comparison of the key divergences between the various points of view more difficult. This fragmentation within the debate suggests the need for a more comprehensive work dealing with issues at a basic level and engaging in explicit comparative analyses.

Second, although it seems initially that we are arguing about the answer to a single question concerning the ends that we ought to strive for, underlying this question are many complex issues that are highly interrelated and difficult to untangle. Should sociologists seek knowledge purely for its own sake, or should they seek it to reach other valued ends? How should the knowledge gained be disseminated? Should sociologists work for one group in society as opposed to others? What overriding goal orientation should the profession choose which would orient and allow evaluation of its activities? What considerations could act as bases for the choice of such an overriding goal orientation and also serve to justify the choice made? Such subissues are complex in themselves and highly interrelated, and although their interrelation is important, some extrication is necessary for the sake of discussion.

Third, perhaps in part because the issues are so complex, and perhaps because we feel so strongly about them, exchange on the issues sometimes seems characterized more by the expression of sentiment and conviction, the hurling of epithets, and a certain sloppiness, than by clarity and well-reasoned argument.

Finally, it seems that even though contexts change, the same arguments are continually rehashed. A change in focus is needed if the debate is to advance.

What we face is an ongoing debate that has existed since the beginnings of sociology, concerning the place and nature of values within the discipline. However, work remains to be done if this debate is to remain fruitful. While preoccupation with self-conscious concerns in any discipline may be debilitating, consideration of what the discipline should value and what direction it should take is useful and necessary.

This book does not presume to resolve the debate, which is and will probably remain ongoing because divergent positions are strongly felt and highly complex. Further, a discipline must continually reassess its goals if it is to remain vital. Rather than attempting to resolve it, this work more modestly hopes to advance the debate by: (1) adding clarity to the presentation of current major positions, (2) suggesting weaknesses within those positions, (3) presenting two contrasting bases for a new position, and (4) offering a position that goes beyond present positions and which might serve as a new focus for the debate.

Since the term *value* plays a major role in the work to follow, a working definition of it is offered. Traditionally there seems to have been a surprisingly high degree of agreement on the meaning of the term in its general usage by professionals most highly involved with it—primarily philosophers, and to a lesser extent social and natural scientists. Frankena (1967, p. 230) suggests that because a high degree of ambiguity or looseness that heavily used terms often engender has crept into the usage, value can best be defined by "keeping to more traditional terms such as 'good' and 'right.' " As a result, we take as a broad working definition of value:

"beliefs about classes of objects, situations, actions, and wholes composed of them in regards to the extent that they are good, right, obligatory, or ought to be." We consider this definition consistent with most traditional uses of the term in philosophy (for example, see Hancock, 1974, pp. 1–11; Frankena, 1967, 1973). Further, although value is seldom explicitly defined when sociologists and other social scientists discuss the role of values in their respective disciplines, this working definition is also consistent with their use of the term. While the working definition is probably satisfactory for most readers, a more extended discussion is offered in the section following Chapter Six on "Value: Uses of the Term." This section discusses key terms within the definition and outlines disagreements on values theory. Also, judgments of value and judgments of obligation, moral and nonmoral value judgments, teleological theories of value justification, valuing as a process, values and preferences, values and attitudes, and the social and systematic nature of values are all considered.

Having considered how the term *value* will be used here, we may turn to the value debate itself. Any understanding of the place of values within sociology must include an understanding of the value-free or value-neutral position. While within the last decade there has been some shift away from the idea that sociology should be extricated from various value stances, there is little doubt that the value-free position has been the dominant one in sociology for the last fifty years. Although the roots of this position can be traced to considerably earlier times, the basis for the value-free position is usually considered to be "Science as a Vocation," a speech presented by Max Weber at Munich University in 1918. At that time, Weber was upset by the practices of *privatdozents*, who were rough German equivalents to U.S. graduate assistants, but who were paid no salary other than the lecture fees received from their students. In particular, he saw the *privatdozents* propounding religious and political views that were calculated to draw crowds rather than to instruct and that were better suited to political or religious leaders than teacher-scientists (Weber, 1946). Further, Weber lived at a time when many faculty members were using the lecture halls as forums to bolster nationalism, monarchy, and various religious beliefs. "When Max Weber began to reflect on his academic vocation, he was appalled by the fact that social sciences were dominated by men who saw it as their patriotic duty to defend the cause of the *Reich* and the Kaiser in their teachings and writings. They oriented their research toward enhancing the fatherland. It was against their prostitution of the scientific calling that Weber directed his shafts" (Coser, 1969, pp. 134–135).

As a result, Weber strongly argued that the social sciences must be directed toward knowledge rather than toward bolstering one's political position. While in a political forum it is quite proper to offer one's position clearly and, as Weber says, to use words as "swords against the enemies," as "weapons," it should be remembered that these words are not at that time tools of scientific analysis. "It would be an outrage, however, to use words in such a fashion in a lecture or in the lecture room" (Weber, 1946, p. 145). Just as the teacher as teacher should remain apolitical, so too should the teacher as scientist, for knowledge is the aim of science, and "whenever the man of science introduces his personal value judgment, a full understanding of the facts ceases" (p. 146). Similarly, men of science must also remain silent on religious issues, and in a sense science must be "irreligious" (p. 142). Weber's stand that social scientists should seek knowledge and avoid personal value judgments is a germinal statement of the more elaborate and explicit value-neutrality positions that have been put forth by more contemporary sociologists.

This contemporary position of sociology being *value free* or *value neutral* is at bottom quite straightforward, and these two terms clearly reflect the nature of the position. This position, put most simply, is that sociology must deal solely with facts and knowledge, be free of value judgments in its practice, and remain neutral concerning the issue of which values ought to be held. Bierstedt offers one of the clearest statements of the position.

> It [sociology] is a science or it is nothing. And in order to be a science it must diligently avoid all pronouncements of an ethical character. As a science it cannot answer questions of value. It can have no traffic with normative statements because there is no logic of the normative. It can deal, as can the other sciences,

only with questions of fact, with propositions, with
statements capable of being true or false. It cannot deal
with questions of good or bad, better or worse, right or
wrong, or any question at all containing the word
"ought." The sociologist, in company with his brother
scientists, has taken seriously the famous remark of
Jeremy Bentham, that the word "ought" ought never to
be used, except in saying that it ought never to be used
[Bierstedt, 1948, p. 310].

What the value-free position presents is the model of the
social scientist who deals strictly with the facts and who does not
enter into the realm of value judgments. Statements in explication
and defense of this position tend to make sweeping generalizations
concerning the place of values in sociology without distinguishing
two separate questions. One question is whether or not values are or
ought to be a part of the body of sociological knowledge. A second
question is whether or not values are or ought to be integral parts of
knowledge seeking and of the profession's orientation to how knowledge is to be used. For example, the value placed upon certain types
and uses of knowledge need not imply that the body of knowledge
is value laden or is value free. The two issues are distinguishable.
A certain physicist may hold strong negative values concerning the
manufacture of nuclear weapons without implying that his knowledge of particle physics is faulty or that the knowledge has values
embedded within it. Bierstedt (1948) and others seem to unjustifi-
ably combine the two issues when sliding from statements such as
"scientists cannot answer questions of value" to general prohibi-
tions that sociologists ought never to use the word *ought*. This work
does not consider the question of whether the body of empirical
knowledge has or ought to have value claims embedded within it.
Rather, it deals only with the question of the place of values in the
process of seeking and employing empirical knowledge.

Coser (1968) suggests that the value-free position and the
idea that sociologists should not enter into the realm of value judgments are dominant in sociology. He cites Ralph Thomlinson's
argument for value-free sociology: "If we want to understand what

makes our social world go round, we must study human behavior with the same detachment as the chemist regarding a reaction in the test tube" (in Coser, 1968, p. 108). While Talcott Parsons would point out differences between sociology and the natural sciences, Coser indicates that Parsons also agrees with this dominant value-free position in sociology.

Not only do those who are sympathetic to the view of value neutrality assume it to be the dominant position in sociology, so do critics such as Gouldner, even though they consider its attainability mythical. "The myth of a value-free sociology has been a conquering one. Today, all the powers of sociology, from Parsons to Lundberg, have entered into a tacit alliance to bind us to the dogma that, 'Thou shalt not commit a value judgment,' especially as sociologists. Where is the sociologist, where is the introductory textbook, the lecture on principles, that does not affirm or imply this rule?" (Gouldner, 1962, p. 199).

Since Gouldner's writing of this statement in 1962, there has been considerable criticism of the position and it no longer has (if it ever had) the unanimous support that Gouldner suggests. Although the majority of sociologists probably still do hold some form of this position, it is unnecessary to argue the proportions. It is sufficient for present purposes to say that the position of value neutrality in sociology continues to be an important one and one that has a large number of adherents.

Relations with Values

In the pure form in which it has been presented, as well as in some of its other formulations, the value-free position seems to suggest that the sociologist should have nothing whatsoever to do with values. Consider, for example, the following implications for the practicing sociologist: "Although all of his evidence indicates that the inequality of the human races is a myth, he would be the first to publish any evidence which would lend scientific support to the biases of a bigot. He does not characterize as evil so fundamental a process as conflict and is not tempted to declare that the abolition of war is a social good. For his is the duty and the responsibility to study social phenomena objectively and without prejudice—without even those prejudices which are on the side of the angels" (Bierstedt, 1948, p. 316).

Does this mean that sociologists must enter into no relations with values in order to legitimately hold a position of value freedom? The several closely related and often conjoined positions discussed in the next few pages suggest that this is not the case.

Study of Values. Although the value-neutral position prohibits the employment of personal values in studying social phenomena or in the use of knowledge produced by that study, this clearly does not prohibit the sociologist from studying the values that people hold. One can maintain a stance of ethical neutrality while studying the values of any culture, subculture, or aggregate of individuals. The position does not prohibit the sociologist from studying what people say ought to be valued, but it does prohibit him from making value judgments concerning the discovered values.

Role Differentiation. Are there no ends which sociologists value—no social problems that sociologists consider to be more than problems for the discipline of sociology? In short, is the sociologist an amoral person? No, it is argued in an accompanying position, one may hold a position of value neutrality for sociology and still remain a moral, ethical, and valuing person; this is possible through *role differentiation.* To be a sociologist is just one of many roles a person plays (or takes), and in that role he acts differently than he would in other roles, such as father, committee chairperson, or friend. Similarly, as for anyone else, he has different expectations placed on him when acting as a sociologist than when taking other roles. While as a sociologist he must remain free of value judgments, there is nothing that prohibits him from expressing or actualizing his values in some other role. For example, the sociologist is free to take value stands as a citizen, as Bierstedt says: "Science and citizenship are two different things. While a given individual may play two different roles, that of scientist and that of citizen, it is of vital importance that he does not try to play them both simultaneously and that the two roles are not confused either by the scientist or by the general public" (1948, p. 313). Therefore, one can take a position of sociological value neutrality and still employ values in other areas of one's life.

Hauser (1969, p. 147) has recently argued along these lines that while taking a position on social, political, or economic issues would compromise sociologists in their basic investigative and educational tasks, sociologists can appropriately "express their value judgments through many other channels without destroying the image of the craft of sociology, [and] dragging sociology as a profession into the heart of the political arena." Since a sociologist can be a good scientist even if he is a naive citizen, "to confuse his roles is to gain nothing while risking his potential to be an effective scientist. It is the task of the sociologist to illuminate rather than to exhort, to analyze rather than to prescribe, to delineate problem areas rather than to confront them" (Hauser, 1969, p. 142). What Hauser and others exhort and prescribe is that sociologists do not have to be value-free people, but they must segment their lives. Although value judgments can quite rightly enter into other segments of their lives, in that segment called "sociology" they should rigorously be excluded.

This segmentation of one's life has been criticized as not allowing sociologists to act as whole persons. Oddly, as Coser points out, it is often those sociologists who explain other areas of social life in terms of role theory (based on role differentiation) who also deny the possibility of role differentiation for sociologists. Further, Coser argues against criticisms of segmentation: "What I have in mind is a tendency in some circles to demand a merging of the role of sociologist with that of citizen; the tendency to assert that anybody who insists on the specificity of the scholar's role is not a full and responsible citizen, or a whole human being. This, I submit, is utter nonsense. I am indeed committed to the calling of sociology, but I have never felt that the discipline claimed more from me than segmental participation. Science is not one of those institutions which claim the total man. I can be a devoted sociologist and a socialist, gardener, or what not" (1969, p. 136). Although there may be disagreement as to the degree to which an individual can successfully differentiate between the roles he plays, there is no doubt that some degree of differentiation is possible and not necessarily unhealthy.*

* Role differentiation is not always easy or possible for all types of roles. Hauser, cited earlier in this section, not only argues for a differ-

Hypothetical Value Statements. The positions related to the basic value-free stance already suggest two ways the sociologist can legitimately stand in relation to values. He may study the values of others, or he may express value judgments in some other role, such as that of citizen. But the question remains, Can the sociologist *as sociologist* deal with value judgments in any other way besides studying them? Yes, he can deal with value judgments in certain prescribed ways if they are not his own. In a sense, he can say that "if this is the goal or value that you hold, then this is the way that you can actualize it." In Weber's words, "*If* you take such and such a stand, then, according to scientific experience, you have to use such and such a *means* in order to carry out your convictions practicably" (1946, p. 151). The sociologist can confront you with the question of whether or not ends are worth the "inevitable means," but he cannot choose between them for you. Weber suggests that each end is attainable through only one necessary, "inevitable" means. However, some sociologists would argue that several alternative means can be suggested for a particular end from which one may choose. By suggesting the means by which others can actualize their values, the sociologist works with value judgments without contradicting a position of value neutrality.

Besides showing how hypothetical goals and values might be achieved, the sociologist can similarly point out the implications of holding certain values. Merton argues that this can be a valuable service: "Not all conditions and processes inimical to the values of men are recognized as such by them. It is the function of the sociol-

---

entiation between the roles of sociologist and citizen, but also between the roles of sociologist and "social engineer." Thus, while he wishes to prohibit sociologists from making value judgments, he sees no difficulty in their doing so as "social engineers." For example, he himself was involved in early stages of the social security system, the Atomic Energy Commission, and public housing and urban renewal programs. Presumably those who hired him as "social engineer" viewed him as a sociologist, and not simply as a bright citizen, and as "social engineer," he probably did research that might be construed as part of the role of the sociologist. Also, he presumably did not carry a set of signs proclaiming "I am now a sociologist" and "I am now a social engineer" to inform those with whom he interacted of what role he was playing. If the sociologist/citizen dichotomy is a difficult one to maintain, clearly the sociologist/social engineer dichotomy is impossible. Incidentally, Hauser offers no warrant for allowing "social engineers" the right to make value judgments while prohibiting sociologists from doing so.

ogist to report the human consequences of holding to certain values and practices, just as it is his function to discover and report the human consequences of departing from the values and practices" (in Coser, 1968, p. 113).

Knowledge for Its Own Sake. A position closely related to that of ethical neutrality is the idea that sociological knowledge should be sought for its own sake, that it is intrinsically valuable. Although this position is often suggested in arguing for value neutrality and objectivity, it is usually modified to suggest that knowledge will be useful in other ways. Merton argues that this conjoining of knowledge as ultimately useful and as intrinsically valuable is an idea that underlies all sciences, not simply the social sciences. He points out that when asked of what use was one of his discoveries, Benjamin Franklin replied, " 'What good is a newborn baby?'—a reply echoed by Pasteur and Faraday in the century to come. This attitude expresses a double confidence: that fundamental scientific knowledge is a self-contained good and that, in any case, it will in due course lead to all manner of practical consequences serving the varied interests of men. There is both an intrinsic and ultimate rationale for basic science" (Merton, 1963, p. 86). The "ultimate benefit" rationale will be covered in a later chapter, but it is important to remember that in practice it is normally presented in conjunction with the idea of knowledge for its own sake. The two are separated here not only for the sake of exposition, but also because they are analytically distinct.

That sociological knowledge is valuable for its own sake is central to the idea of value neutrality in two ways. First, it supports the neutrality position, for it allows the exclusion of all other ends or values which sociology might strive toward. If all other ends or values are excluded, and knowledge is not maintained to be intrinsically of value, it would be impossible to argue that sociology itself is of value and should therefore be supported. The assumption that sociological knowledge is a self-contained good provides a rationale for maintaining that the enterprise can be freed from other values and still be legitimately pursued. Second, the intrinsic value of knowledge further supports ethical neutrality, which can be of value, for it is said to lead to sociological knowledge. Thus, value neutrality is of instrumental value in leading to the intrinsic good of knowledge, due to the way the knowledge process is conceived and the way values may interfere with that process:

> Human beings are seen as being essentially passive receptors of the reality experienced through their senses. Knowledge of what we consider to be external reality is something that happens to us. It happens best when the only inner desire that motivates our attention is our unfettered curiosity, that is, a concern for knowing reality in terms that are independent of any other concern. Thus we are exhorted to practice what is called "pure science," the search for the truth for its own sake, which is regarded as an intrinsically valuable activity. In the context of this search, our voluntary activities must be restricted to actions which allow us to observe phenomena that concern us while interfering with them as little as possible. In other words, we must become passive receptors, doing only whatever is necessary to let reality speak for itself [Biblarz, 1969, p. 2].*

Thus, knowledge is seen as a product of value neutrality, which allows sociological knowledge to remain of value while other values are removed.

As pointed out earlier, the position that knowledge is intrinsically valuable and ought to be sought for its own sake is seldom offered in pure form—probably because it is difficult to present a strong and convincing argument in its favor. Arguments could be mustered for knowledge for its own sake, such as, "it is exciting," or "it makes our lot in life easier to bear if we understand it," or "it makes one a whole person." Such arguments suggest that there are other values that are placed above knowledge—and which knowledge is instrumental in achieving—and thus knowledge is not truly sought for its own sake. In fact, it is some other end which is

---

* This statement by Biblarz is generally a fair representation of the conception of knowledge and its relation to other concerns or values. However, it probably also overemphasizes passivity in knowledge processes, an overemphasis which leads to the criticism that knowledge cannot be acquired totally passively. The overemphasis stems from the failure to distinguish between two types of activity: activity aimed solely at gathering knowledge and activity that is directed toward ends other than knowledge ("action").

sought, and the question as to whether it can be attained by knowledge or can better be reached through some other means still remains unanswered.

Ultimately, the idea that sociological knowledge ought to be sought for its own sake is probably best considered an assertion or assumption based on the belief that knowledge is intrinsically valuable. It is best considered an assumption for: (1) if one argues that its value is derived from something extrinsic to it, it is no longer intrinsically valued; and (2) if one argues that it is intrinsically valuable because something intrinsic to it is valuable, then the argument is tautological. However, as suggested earlier, the knowledge for its own sake position is important for both understanding and assessing the merits of the value-neutral position.

To assess those merits we must ask: Is sociology really free of values other than the value of knowledge for its own sake, or can it be, or ought it to be? To the extent that sociology is oriented toward values or directed toward ends other than sociological knowledge, we can say that it is not now value free or value neutral. To the same extent that sociology is likely in the future to seek ends other than pure sociological knowledge, it is also likely in the future not to be free of values.

Two

Relevance of Values
for Sociology

Given the difficulties involved in holding a value-free or value-neutral position in sociology, it will be argued that such a position is unacceptable for several reasons. While a strict interpretation of the term *value free* may imply that sociology ought to be free of all values, this is clearly not the intent of those who argue for the value-free position. To elaborate, sociology may be conceived of as an imperfect body of knowledge. It is quite consistent with this position to hold one of two types of values: a metavalue of truth seeking (the perfection of that body of knowledge) or a value of seeking knowledge according to the discipline's conception of truth. Thus, it would seem unfair and inaccurate to criticize someone holding a position of value freedom who claims that she values sociological knowledge or that she values one method of inquiry more than another because it seems more likely to increase sociological knowledge. It seems equally unreasonable to demand that a sociologist maintaining this position be totally free of all extrinsic values or that she prove that the profession be free of values, just as it is unreasonable to ask her to prove that the body of sociological knowledge will be perfected. It does, however, seem reasonable to criticize this position if sociology is, and seems likely to remain, *not* value free to a significant degree.

In particular, the body of sociological knowledge is not the product of values that are solely intrinsic to it. Rather, it is a product of knowledge processes that are, and will probably continue to be, directed by extrinsic values. Also, the use of sociological knowledge is not directed by neutral values. In short, knowledge is sought and employed to ends other than pure knowledge. To the extent that these claims are true, sociology is not and is not likely to be value free.* It is therefore argued that the value-free position as it is currently expressed inaccurately reflects current and probable future sociology and inadequately deals with extrinsic value orientations that are likely to remain in sociology.†

* Although, as Dewey and Humber (1966, p. 647) point out, there is a group of writers who argue that social scientists *"will, inescapably,* make such value judgments," here it is argued only that they are *likely* to do so with high probability. Arguing that sociologists must make value judgments implies that there is something inherent in sociology that demands them. Any such argument would probably at best be a tautology, where the necessity of value judgments is derived from the chosen definition of sociology. Just as it was conceded that it seems unreasonable to demand that it be demonstrated that sociology can be completely freed of values, it seems equally unreasonable to demand proof that sociology must always employ value judgments.

† Most simply, the position to be presented holds that although the employment of nonepistemic values in sociology could cease at some future date, this seems unlikely; therefore these values must be dealt with. The nature of the argument can be made clear by an analogy to sexual relations. Although everyone at some future time could decide not to indulge in sex, it seems highly unlikely. Given the existence of sexual relations now and its high probability in the future, a prescription not to engage in sexual relations would not only reflect present and future behavior inadequately but would also be of little use in deciding what are the best means of sexual expression.

Extrinsic Values Employed in the Knowledge Process

The number of ways of seeking knowledge that are open to the sociologist may be delimited on the basis of knowledge concerns, such as the state of the body of sociological knowledge or the means believed likely to lead to knowledge. However, such intrinsic pure knowledge values can usually only eliminate some of the alternatives available; choosing among the remaining possibilities demands reference to other personally or socially held value judgments.

For example, one must choose a general problem area from the extremely large number of problems encompassed by the boundaries of sociology. Sociological theory as well as the available data both suggest and limit the number of general problem areas (such as the nature of conflict, social structure and social process, and social order) that ought to be investigated. Yet, as even a sociologist who defends the value-neutral position would suggest, they do not fully delimit the alternatives, and "of those that are susceptible to scientific explanation, it is a matter of nonscientific decision that some ought to be investigated first and others at a later and more propitious time" (Bierstedt, 1948, p. 318). Other value judgments must be employed, for at a given time many issues will be viewed by the individual sociologist or the profession as being of equal theoretical importance. Also, it is no simple matter to determine the relative importance of each possible problem area to the body of knowledge as a whole, and as a result the choice between them is more a function of external values than of carefully weighing their import to and impact on the knowledge system.

Similarly, once a general problem area is chosen it may be translated into an extremely large number of substantive areas, and these alternatives are only partially delimited by methodological concerns and theoretical applicability. Choosing to seek knowledge in the area of race relations rather than sex roles, creativity rather than conformity, the sociology of religion rather than the sociology of work, or any choice between such disparate areas as social stratification, the family, the sociology of war, and criminology demands value judgments that are not implied by pure knowledge concerns.

Which general method or particular technique is chosen in seeking sociological knowledge is also only partly determined by such pure knowledge concerns as the ability of the sociologist to meet the assumptions of the method or the extent to which the method is believed likely to lead to "truth." Again, many options may be scientifically satisfactory, and the choice between them must be made on the basis of other values. Often a method is chosen according to extrinsic concerns, such as the use to which the knowledge will likely be put. Thus, while theoretical concerns may be satisfied by numerous methods with fairly low degrees of generalizability, one method offering greater generalizability may be chosen if the applicability of the findings is a major concern. Similarly, a level of significance which is more stringent than that demanded by simple theory testing may be chosen if confidence in the findings is important for extratheoretical reasons (as is the case in testing drugs).

In fact, not only are extrinsic values often necessary in choosing methods and techniques, they are often given priority over pure knowledge values. Consider this statement by Gray (1968, p. 179) offered in another connection: "But one should note that German physicians who systematically froze human beings in tubs of ice, and, in the conduct of sterilization experiments, sent electrical charges through female ovaries were quite useful to the Nazi regime. While some of these examples might seem extreme, one must recognize nonetheless that the behavior of these German scientists falls quite within the limits of the value free model offered."

While Gray is quite correct in pointing out that the value-free position does not judge such methods of gaining knowledge, it is equally instructive to remember that the vast majority of sociologists would not perform similar research even if their societies allowed them to. Similarly, while it has been suggested that a difficulty for sociology is the inability to conduct many societal-level experiments that would provide important data because the experiments are prohibited by society (Nagel, 1961, pp. 450–451), many sociologists would not perform many of these tests due to their value commitments even if they could. Thus, on many occasions the method most clearly suggested by pure knowledge concerns is ruled out by other value judgments made by the sociologist. In the case of the choice of methods, then, not only is the sociologist not value neutral, but certain value judgments are given precedence over knowledge concerns. If this were not the case, any method of seeking knowledge would be preferred to forgoing that knowledge, even if a particular method entailed death, suffering, or the violation of some other deeply held value.

At a more general level, the code of ethics of the American Sociological Association suggests that many extraepistemic values are given precedence over knowledge concerns. Some values that are stated or implied in the code are that the sociologist should (1) respect the right of privacy of subjects, (2) respect the right of confidentiality of subjects, (3) avoid personal harm to subjects, and (4) avoid misinterpretation of his abilities (abstracted from Dorn and Long, 1974, p. 33). If ethical prescriptions such as these are taken seriously, presumably one would not violate them even at the expense of knowledge. For example, sociologists should "refuse to accept grants or contracts if such an acceptance would mean violation of ethical principles" (Dorn and Long, 1974, p. 33). It would seem here that an ethical principle is given precedence before knowledge—certainly it is given an equal status with epistemic values.

Extraepistemic values are also involved in choosing how to disseminate knowledge. It may be argued that the future growth of the body of knowledge dictates that new information should be published in certain sociological journals rather than others because their readerships are most likely to elaborate and extend this knowledge. However, the decision of whether to disseminate the information and theory to a wider audience must also be made—a choice that cannot be made without referring to values extrinsic to the information itself. Clearly, the decision to insure that a particular group, such as the military, a governmental body, or persons on welfare, is given access to sociological information also demands reference to extraepistemic values. Further, even the decision of whether to disseminate research findings within the discipline (consider the Jensen, 1969, study of black IQ) must consider the possibility of the results of the findings becoming generally known outside the discipline. In short, there are many choices that must be made concerning dissemination of the body of knowledge that the body of knowledge cannot dictate.

It may be argued that the epistemological process within sociology demands that nonepistemic values be included if knowledge is to be effectively sought. First, it has been argued forcefully (primarily by those of a phenomenological and ethnomethodological bent) that gaining valid sociological knowledge of all kinds, in particular of experience, demands subjective involvement with those studied; this means that the sociologist adopts and shares the meanings, interests, and values of the studied group. According to this view, then, the sociologist must adopt a set of values in the pursuit of knowledge, and it seems likely that a large number of sociologists will continue to do this. (While a large number of sociologists could be cited who support this view, a clear presentation of the arguments is found in Phillips, 1971, particularly pp. 124–160).

Second, while Biblarz was cited in Chapter One as pointing out that the value-free position rests on a passive conception of the knowledge process, he also states that there exists an alternative, more active view of how the knowledge process operates. "This alternative view sees humans as entities which exist in an environment with which they continuously interact, so that they are never passive receptors of experience. Reality is discovered in the context of acting within it for human (that is, value laden) purposes and human beings learn about the world by changing it or failing to change it; in the process they also change themselves" (1969, p. 3).

This view of the epistemological process does not seem unreasonable, and as a result sociologists are likely to recognize that sociological knowledge is not the result of simple passive receptivity, but of sociological action. If knowledge continues to be sought by means of action, that is, behavior that is directed by values and value actualization, extraepistemic values are likely to play a very significant role in the knowledge process.

To summarize, at innumerable points in the knowledge process at which decisions are likely to be made, extraepistemic value judgments must be relied upon. It could be argued that many of these decisions are based not so much on beliefs about what is right or good, but on the basis of other factors, such as simple personal preference, habit, convenience, or conformity to social convention. Thus, for example, the decision of an individual sociologist to disseminate knowledge through a particular journal may be due to previous success in getting articles published, the journal's prestige, or the fact that respected colleagues have published in it. While it may be admitted that factors such as these are not, strictly speaking, value judgments, this does not seriously weaken the line of reasoning as a whole. First, while such factors may influence many of these personal decisions, higher level value questions also usually play a major role in legitimating these factors (for example, the question of the value of the social conventions, or personal preferences)'. Second, while value judgments may not be made every time a decision is made, at some point basic questions, such as the value of disseminating information to a wider public, must be addressed. Third, such decision making does not take place solely, or perhaps even primarily, at the level of the individual, but rather at the level of the profession as a whole and its major subgroups. This decision making usually demands evaluation that cannot be considered merely a summation of personal preferences; it takes into account a valuation of future professional directions. Even professional conventions do not remain eternally unchallenged; from time to time they are evaluated and then either justified and strengthened or found unjustified and modified or rejected.

Further, while various parts of the knowledge process have been treated separately for the sake of exposition, it should be noted that the parts of the knowledge process are interdependent, and choices made on the basis of value judgments will be reflected in other parts of the knowledge process as well. Since the value-free position must necessarily abstain from the choice of extraepistemic values, it is useless in evaluating these choices. It is similarly inapplicable in determining the uses of sociological knowledge once obtained.

Values and the Use of Sociological Knowledge

As the body of sociological knowledge becomes increasingly refined, the possibilities for its use and application also increase. To the extent that this knowledge is used or applied, choices are made which involve extraepistemic values. It is argued here as in the preceding section on the processes of seeking knowledge that the value-neutral position neither reflects nor adequately deals with the situation.

Necessary to the application of sociological knowledge is the ability to control. Again, in order to accurately represent the value-neutral position, we must make a general distinction between the two major senses in which the term *control* is used. The first sense is that which we normally encounter in introductory textbooks describing the goals of science as "explanation, prediction, and control." In this sense the ability to control phenomena is sought not for its own sake but in order to test the accuracy of a theory or hypothesis. If phenomena can be manipulated in a manner in accordance with a theory, it can be said that one's explanation probably has some validity. If a sociologist uses control in this way, we can say that her actions are dictated by epistemic concerns and that she has not violated the value-free stance.

However, if the sociologist controls phenomena for some end other than the testing of theory, she is no longer following the dictates of value neutrality. In this second sense, then, the term *control* refers to the manipulation of a phenomenon either by changing it from its present state or by consciously preserving its present state in light of some other valued end. Henceforth it is in this latter sense that the term *control* will be used unless clearly specified.

Of course, the two types of control are not unrelated. When control as a test of theory improves, so does the possibility of using knowledge in ways not dictated by knowledge values. It is perhaps for this reason, coupled with the recognition of the growth of the body of sociological knowledge, that concern has been expressed (as we shall see on the following pages) over the misuse of sociological knowledge and its resulting control capabilities. Although there is considerable disagreement over what constitutes misuse, there certainly seems to be a unifying concern about the ends to which sociological knowledge is used.

It is not argued here that knowledge will likely be *misused,* for what constitutes misuse depends upon the orientation of the evaluator. It is simply argued that sociological knowledge is likely to be *used,* and that the decisions about when to use sociological knowledge imply value choices, even if they are not made explicit.

Before proceeding, it should be pointed out that one may feel that any concern over the use of sociological knowledge may be premature or exaggerated, since it has not matured sufficiently to enable any significant degree of control. Bauer (1965) makes this point in reference to discussions of social responsibility within psychology, claiming that psychologists overstate their actual or potential power to manipulate human behavior. Citing examples of overstatement in discussions of brainwashing and Packard's *The Hidden Persuaders* (1957), Bauer argues that while there are dangers of abuse of psychological knowledge, they should not be exaggerated so as to breed fear of unrealistic dangers.* He suggests that psychologists should be "responsibly responsible" rather than "pseudo-responsible"; that is, discussions should deal with realistic rather than fanciful dangers (Bauer, 1965).

Similarly, discussions of the potential misuses of sociological knowledge may be overstated as they have been in psychology. Although one might contend that in both disciplines there is little danger of being overcautious, Bauer (p. 51) counters that there are several ill effects of such discussions. "The furor over 'hidden persuasion' created a market for a considerable amount of bad research. . . . The result of this, in turn, was to create disillusion and confusion in the ranks of laymen who had contact with this research. Visions of the use of the social sciences for totalitarian control have caused us difficulties in the halls of Congress. Perhaps more serious and general is the impact of such discussions on reinforcement of the public image of psychologists as dangerous and untrustworthy."

However, Bauer himself overstates the negative impact of these discussions "in the halls of Congress" and elsewhere. While there is a danger of creating unfounded fear through overstatement, sociological and psychological knowledge is, and will in all probability continue to be, used. Sociological control capabilities, while clearly not Orwellian in nature, and while in infancy compared with control capabilities of the natural sciences, will be refined and should be recognized. Further, even given that current control capabilities are comparatively limited in all the social sciences, "the issue of the control of behavior must be put into a broader time perspective. . . . If we put our research efforts in the longer context of the age

* Bauer (1965, p. 51) suggests an interesting, if undocumented, explanation of the motivation for these discussions: "The only interpretation that I can put on the preference for the discussion of fanciful over realistic dangers is that they must serve some special need which, in turn, I infer to be enhancement of our egos as psychologists *via* an image of potential omnipotence."

of the earth, the age of man, the age of psychology as a science, then it would seem clear that the scientific information required for effective behavior control will probably be a reality in a relatively short period of time, be it 10, 20, or 100 years" (Krasner, 1965, p. 12).

In addition, even if the time span for "effective behavior control" is deemed distant, sociological knowledge may now be used for extradisciplinary ends even if it is highly imperfect and its effectiveness quite limited.

The idea of putting sociological knowledge to use is not a recent one; it has been argued that the early sociologists sought sociological knowledge in order to use it for what they considered to be the betterment of society. Braude views the history of sociology in this way: "Sociology was born out of the desire to protest as well as discover. The Wards, the Simmels, the Parks, and even the Webers, could not see knowledge apart from action; the *vita contemplativa* was coterminous with the *vita activa*" (1964, p. 397). Many sociologists of the next generation also saw sociology as producing usable knowledge, perceived themselves as social engineers, and founded such journals as *Social Hygiene* (1916), in which sociological knowledge was applied to issues of "social health and morality."

More recently, Lynd, in his now famous book *Knowledge for What?* (1948), renewed the call for sociological knowledge to be used directly to deal with social ills. Lundberg (1947), while considerably more positivistic than Lynd and differing in other significant ways, also urged that sociology to be applied to solving social problems in *Can Science Save Us?* Even Bierstedt, after arguing strongly for the value-free and role differentiation positions presented earlier, surprisingly concludes that sociology should be used for extraepistemic purposes:

> Finally, it is time for the scientist to acknowledge that the ultimate test of his activity lies in the social use and consequence of his conclusions. Whatever freedom the sociologist may achieve from the exigencies of time and circumstance, it is still important, and now more than ever before, to narrow the gap between the

discovery of new principles and their application to
the sphere of human relations. Society should not be
the victim of a cultural lag between sociological knowledge and social use. No scientific scruples, therefore, as
important as those scruples are, should delay a con-
stantly increasing sensitivity to the social role of social
science [1948, pp. 318–319].

The calls for sociological knowledge to be used or to be
developed so that it can be put to use are still heard and are likely
to continue. Tarter (1973), for example, calls for increasing work
in the area of developing social technologies and for sociologists to
become social technologists. The goal is a planned society, with behavior changes in "desired" directions. Unfortunately, Tarter, like
most of his predecessors, neglects to inform his readers to what ends
the society is planned for or what the desired directions of social
changes are. He nonetheless proudly proclaims that "not only will
the social technologist be part experimental psychologist, he will
also be part architect. Techniques of social intervention will be
aimed primarily at direct management of environmental dimensions
of human existence" (p. 157).

Articles and books such as those mentioned, which proclaim
that sociological knowledge ought to be sought for its usefulness
and then employed, may no longer be necessary. Sociological knowledge is already being sought and used by both sociologists themselves
and others outside of sociology. There is increasing recognition that
sociologists are seeking employable knowledge and using their
knowledge for a wide variety of purposes. It is not surprising that
those who are most vocal and insistent about the extent to which
sociologists are employing knowledge for extradisciplinary ends are
those who are critical of the values that direct its use. Birnbaum
(1971, p. 734) points out that the primary political criticism of
sociology comes from the left. "Sociology in its present form has
irreducible ideological components. . . . These ideological components are closely related to political elements: sociologists have
become ancillary agents of power, by performing intelligence service
for purposes of domination, exploitation, and manipulation."

Thus, sociologists are seen as using techniques for gathering information in the service of elites that can be used to directly maintain the established order by agencies and corporations for which the sociologists are employed, act as consultants, or do solicited research. "Henceforth the inspiration of sociology will always be more responsive to the social demand for a nationalist practice to serve bourgeois ends: money, profit, and the maintenance of order. Evidence abounds. Industrial sociology seeks above all the adjustment of the worker to his job. The possibility of any other approach is limited, since the sociologist who receives a salary from management must respect the goal of the economic system: to produce as much as possible in order to make as much money as possible" (Cohn-Bendit and others, 1968, p. 544).

Cohn-Bendit and others also offer additional evidence of sociologists seeking knowledge that they view as serving bourgeois and nationalist ends, such as propaganda research in political sociology, Stouffer's *The American Soldier* (1949), and research for the advertising industry.

Regardless of whether one agrees with the values that determine the use for which sociological knowledge is sought, it often does seem to be sought for specific application. While directly applicable knowledge probably is sought to an even greater extent in the natural sciences, the sciences in general have emphasized applied over basic research. Bendix (1970, p. 840) reports that in the United States in 1966, $3.2 billion were spent on basic research, while $18.9 billion were spent on applied research and development. Presumably, sociology in the future, after a sufficient expansion of its knowledge base, will approximate the proportion of applied to basic research of the natural sciences. (Of course this does not mean that basic knowledge cannot be obtained when doing applied research, but it does mean that applicability criteria must be satisfied for a project to be funded as "applied.") There seems even now to be an increase in the number of research grants that are requested or solicited by granting agencies (as opposed to those submitted unsolicited by sociologists).

To return to the leftist critique, it is argued that sociologists do not merely seek knowledge that is useful, but that they seek knowledge that is specifically useful to the establishment. This, it is claimed, is due to the fact that either sociologists agree with establishment values, or more benignly, that only the establishment can adequately finance the knowledge process: "The profession as a whole is primarily geared to the service of existing power. Most sociologists have learned to do research that depends on the availability of relatively large sums of money, and it is obvious that these sums cannot come from the poor" (Biblarz, 1969, p. 4).

In addition to seeking knowledge that is useful to those in power, sociologists are charged by critics with actively using that knowledge themselves. As openings for sociologists increase in agencies, industry, and research organizations that deal with social planning, sociologists are actively employing sociological knowledge more extensively than before. Thus, Gray (1968, p. 180) argues that sociologists who profess value freedom have really become "professional hand maidens of the going value system. . . . No longer truly intellectual, they have assumed a new role as employees, consultants, or technicians serving the present establishment." As a result, Gray suggests remedial action by having the sociologist suggest policy.* Put most simply, critics see sociologists who employ sociological knowledge as intellectual policemen. This description might be applied most appropriately to those involved in evaluation research, where the primary goal is to determine the effectiveness of a social program on some target population in achieving goals set by those who implemented the program. Caro (1969, p. 88), who is sympathetic to evaluation research, acknowledges this characterization, but points out that evaluation researchers themselves consider it to be inaccurate:

> Where action programs are carried out by a
> formal organization, evaluative research is most com-

---

* Oddly, in attempting to show that one can make value judgments and remain scholarly, Gray (1968, p. 180) suggests the following, apparently as a legitimate way in which to employ values in guiding social policy: "Likewise, if the social scientist sees in his data an impending racial crisis is he (or his data? or sociology? or science?) in any way compromised should he attempt to convince the city authorities to take certain measures for the good of all urban residents concerned? Obviously not. To be responsible has always been a virtue!" Undoubtedly, some black radicals would not consider this stance too far removed from being a "professional hand maiden of the going value system."

monly sponsored by external funding sources and/or top administrators. . . . Those who actually carry out programs to be evaluated tend to be subordinate to those to whom evaluative researchers report. Although this structural arrangement puts the evaluation researcher in the same organizational position as an inspector or a policeman, evaluative researchers insist their role is quite different. Thus Likert and Lippit emphasize ". . . that the objective of the research is to discover the relative effectiveness of different methods and principles and that the study is in no way an attempt to perform a policing function. The emphasis must be on discovering what principles work best and why, and not on finding and reporting which individuals are doing their jobs well or poorly."

Despite emphasis on principles in the research, the principles that work and those people who act upon them or actualize them are not readily separable. Suppose two agencies employ two markedly different operating principles, and according to some agreed upon criteria agency A is more effective than agency B in bringing about desired changes in the target population. We might conclude that the operating principle of agency A is more effective. However, it is also possible that the operating principle of agency B is equally effective, but the staff of agency B is not as well qualified, motivated, or productive. At some point, responsibility for the failure or success must be laid primarily on either the principles or the individuals, and thus the individuals must also be evaluated.

More importantly, this whole argument misses the more significant point of who is being policed. The really problematic policing occurs on the action program's target population, not its staff. "Discovering what principles work best and why" means what works best to change the behavior of the target population in ways desired by external funding sources. Being a policeman in this sense is not necessarily undesirable; it depends on the extent to which one accepts the values that the action program represents.

In fact, sociologists are increasingly entering professions that involve evaluation research and other functions that are not purely epistemic, precisely because they share the values of the action programs. Thus, a review of the literature finds that one of the two major reasons (the other being that theoretically important hypotheses can often be tested) emphasized by social scientists for doing evaluative research is that "the social action goals of some social scientists parallel those of their clients; and their belief in the potential contribution of scientific evaluation to the development of effective programs leads to involvement" (Caro, 1969, p. 89). For example, many such researchers express an interest in such target populations as the aged, the mentally ill, and alcoholics.*

It should be pointed out that persons employing sociological knowledge do not always do so in the most commonly expected ways. For example, while evaluation researchers are often accused of maintaining the status quo, they are often desirous of change and perform their research to that end. "Researchers often have a vested interest in discovering inefficiency and encouraging change. . . . In part, the social scientists justify their claim to superior knowledge of human affairs by dramatizing inadequacies in conventional wisdom and existing programs. . . . Evaluating scientists are thus predisposed to see the need for change" (Caro, 1969, p. 89).

Similarly unexpected is the fact that many self-proclaimed radicals have recently carried out research and taken positions within established systems in order to modify the systems according to their own values (see Colfax, 1970, p. 82).

Although many would debate the justifiability of the values involved, many activities could be cited as further evidence that sociologists have been employing sociological knowledge to implement valued ends. Project Camelot, funded by the Army's Special Operations Research Office, is a famous and controversial example. That project sought "first, to devise procedures for assessing the

---

* It may be interesting to note the reasons suggested in the literature as to why administrators of action programs wish evaluative research done. Stated reasons offered are (1) introducing greater rationality into the decision-making process, (2) feedback to other administrators for program refinement, (3) dissemination of program information to the public, and (4) providing accounting information to funding agencies. Covert reasons are (1) aid in settling an internal dispute, (2) justification of previous decisions, (3) support of an attempt to gain power, (4) justification of postponement of action, (5) placing responsibility for decisions outside the organization, and (6) lending an aura of prestige to the program (abstracted from Caro, 1969, p. 89).

potential for internal war within national societies; second, to identify with increased degrees of confidence, those actions which a government might take to relieve conditions which are assessed as giving rise to a potential for internal war" (Horowitz, 1977, p. 226). Sociologists are increasingly employed to seek knowledge that will be useful for reaching organizational objectives. This can be seen in the growing numbers of sociologists employed by government, the military, and private industry. Even within academic settings, sociologists are increasingly labeling themselves "applied sociologists," and areas of specialty as well as whole departments of applied sociology are emerging. Also sociologists continue to join professional organizations expressly devoted to the attainment of valued ends. The Society for the Study of Social Problems (SSSP) is such an organization. In their call for papers for their twenty-seventh annual meeting in 1977 the society's commitment was made clear: "From the beginning, SSSP has worked from two premises about the study of social problems. The first was that the analysis of the problems of our society and the treatments they receive is a fundamental way of understanding the character of the society itself. The second was that bending our best efforts to dealing with those problems is a basic obligation, reason and justification for our work and for our special position as students and scholars." Many journals are also making explicit value commitments that extend well beyond dissemination of sociological knowledge. More evidence could easily be mustered, but perhaps the point is amply made.

In short, sociologists are both seeking knowledge and actively applying it in order to actualize a wide range of values. The fact that there is such wide disagreement about the values that guide the use of sociological knowledge suggests more strongly that the values are nonepistemic. These nonepistemic uses of sociological knowledge by sociologists seem likely to continue. There is no reason to assume that sociologists will not see problems in their various societies to which their knowledge can be applied. Further, as laymen increasingly recognize sociological knowledge and sociological expertise as useful, they will increasingly pressure sociologists to actively employ their knowledge. At present, while the results of attempted use of social scientific knowledge is sometimes disappointing, "a report of the National Science Foundation acknowledges that social scientists are being called upon at unprecedented rates to provide solutions to pressing national and local problems" (Tarter, 1973, p. 154).

As long as sociologists continue to use their knowledge, they will employ a set of values; thus, as description, the value-free position is inaccurate. Further, as long as sociologists continue to use their knowledge, the value-free position is prescriptively of little value, since it contributes nothing to the crucial question of which values should be actualized.

Use of Sociological Knowledge by Nonsociologists

It may be asked, however, What if sociologists in the future completely ceased seeking knowledge for reasons other than for its own sake and consistently refused to use this knowledge? Would sociology not then be value free? Even if we grant for the moment this unlikely possibility, only the *sociologists* could be considered free of values, and not necessarily *sociology*. Sociology is not simply those who practice it, it is also a body of knowledge. Even if sociologists decided against using this knowledge for valued ends, the question still remains of whether it will be used by others—of whether it will remain free of value employment.

Let us assume that the body of sociological knowledge is value neutral. This would not preclude its use in the actualization of widely divergent and often contradictory values. Also, regardless of the nature of a person's values, the knowledge can be employed by anyone who is aware of its potential usefulness in achieving his ends and has access to the resources required for its implementation. "The sciences are neutral in terms of theoretical knowledge but are not neutral in the consequences resulting from the practical application of that knowledge—which could be manipulated for positive and constructive or negative and destructive ends. As Bertrand Russell made clear: 'Science in so far as it consists of knowledge, must be regarded as having value, but in so far as it consists of techniques the question whether it is to be praised or blamed depends upon the use that is made of the technique' " (Vrga, 1971, p. 247).

Thus, ideally, the value-free sociologist produces knowledge that can be used by anyone in the service of any valued ends. The implications of this aspect of the value-free position are suggested by Gray: "Should the full impact of Lundberg's observation that physical scientists are not as severely disturbed by political upheaval not be appreciated, he stated more precisely the virtue of his position for one concerned with the survival or success of his individual career: 'The service of *real* (that is, value free) social scientists would be indispensible to Fascists or Communists or Democrats, just as are the services of physicists and physicians'" (Gray, 1968, p. 179).

In this situation, the body of sociological knowledge is analogous to the body of a prostitute—it is used by anyone and in a wide variety of ways. The analogy breaks down in that the sociologist producing the knowledge would ideally not be directly compensated financially for services rendered. Not only can the body of sociological knowledge be used, even if not by sociologists, but there is also an extremely high probability that it will be used as various segments of society recognize its potential usefulness in attaining their own ends. Its use will increase still further as it is refined and instances of its successful employment are recognized and become more plentiful. There seems little reason to think that the world will become a less problematic place in which to live than it was in 1948. "Insistent public dilemmas clamor for solution. Decisions will be made and public policies established—because no delaying or turning back is possible in this hurrying climactic era. If the social scientist is too bent on 'waiting until all the data are in,' or if university policies warn him off controversial issues, the decisions will be made anyway—without him. They will be made by the 'practical' man and by the 'hard headed politician,' chivvied* by interest and pressure blocks" (Lynd, 1948, p. 9).

Thus, even if sociologists free themselves of values in using sociology, it does not seem likely that sociological knowledge will be freed from value employment.† Sociological knowledge, and thus

---

* "Chivvied"?!

† Not only will sociological knowledge be used in accordance with values, it will also probably be used to change the values of others. This is often the case in "mission" oriented programs (that is, poverty, mental health, and so on), where the necessary first step is to change the values of the target population to correspond to those of the persons running the program. Andrew (1967, p. 89) puts it this way:

sociology, are not freed from an intimate connection with values. Yet the question still remains of whether sociologists share in any responsibility for the use of the knowledge they produce. It is argued here that they do *because* they produce it (unless they do so under duress), just as the weapons manufacturer incurs an indirect responsibility when his weapons are used. Further, "scientific research is expensive and society must divert resources from other needs to support it. By accepting support, the sociologist incurs an obligation to reciprocate" (Kultgen, 1970, p. 186).

Thus, the minimum one could suggest is that the sociologist has the responsibility, even if he is able himself to avoid the use of knowledge, to act as watchdog concerning its use by others. In an editorial in *Science,* Abelson (1970, p. 241) argues for this role:

> Others have pointed out that once facts have become generally known, the scientist can no longer determine how his discoveries may be applied. To some degree this argument is valid. Nevertheless, scientists will have continuing and important roles in determining how science is applied. One important function is that of watchdog.
>
> In exploiting scientific discoveries, humanity will squander resources and unwittingly conduct profoundly important experiments on itself and its environment. Who will evaluate such experiments and be alert to emerging problems? The man on the street can scarcely fill such a role. Government might, but its leadership is in the hands of the politicians who rarely act until an issue is crystallized by others. Scientists or engineers in government service might act as watch-

---

This problem [of nonshared goals in a program] is expressed, for example, in the statements that "middle class values" of the programmers are not necessarily held by those for whom the project is provided. In that instance the manipulator has to intervene in the value constellation of the population prior to other attempts to change the condition of that population. In some sense this interplay of values is involved in most applied programs designed to alleviate social problems and the individuals served by the program are under constant pressure to adopt the goals of the practitioners.

dogs, but in general, politicians prefer that bureaucrats speak only when spoken to. Employees in industry are in much the same circumstance. Thus, academic scientists and scientific societies have responsibilities that they cannot escape.

But even to perform this minimal role of watchdog, the individual scientist or scientific society needs a set of values or an overriding goal orientation in order to decide when to bark and when to remain silent. It is difficult to be an effective watchdog without knowing what one is watching for. The value-neutral position cannot help us with this problem.

Hopefully it is clear that sociology is, and in all probability will continue to be, highly involved with extraepistemic values. While we may disagree with Bennis concerning the lack of literature in this area, we may nonetheless agree with his final conclusion: "The social scientist's own value system is a topic, it hardly needs saying, that we pay scant attention to, except for some rather bored and pious statements about how value free we are, a statement that seems more empirically free than anything else" (1968, p. 242).

At numerous points in the knowledge process choices are necessary that often involve extraepistemic values. Further, sociologists are increasingly using knowledge and directly seeking knowledge so that it might be used, which again involves extraepistemic value choices. Finally, even if sociologists somehow managed not to employ sociological knowledge, it would likely be used by others in accordance with their own values.* As Benne (1965, p. 6) suggests,

---

* We might even go further in this argument, contending that even if sociologists did not employ sociological knowledge for certain ends, and even if others did not directly employ that knowledge, sociology still would not be freed of the necessity of choosing value orientations. This is because the process of seeking knowledge often creates changes in the phenomena studied (even if these changes are not sought) which may or may not be valued. Even in the physical sciences—usually offered as models of detachment—the idea that the scientist is merely an observer has had to be abandoned:

> Increasingly, the scientist creates the universe which he studies. Physicists are producing particles unknown in nature. Chemists have produced elements unknown in nature

this is the case for all the sciences: "Whether we have achieved formats, methods, and value orientations for an adequate *integration* of scientific and non-scientific resources is problematic. That the *desegregation* of scientific and non-scientific personnel has been widely and unevenly achieved, is a fact" (Benne, 1965, p. 6). Thus, the real question confronting sociology is not *whether* to include an extraepistemic value orientation, but *which* extraepistemic value orientation should be chosen.

At the beginning of this chapter it was stated that it would not be argued that sociologists will *inescapably* make value judgments. Rather, the more difficult but more realistic position was taken that sociology is *to an important degree* not value free. By making this qualification, we have not completely ruled out the possibility of value freedom. In other words, an adherent to a value-free position might argue, "Since value freedom or neutrality is still a *possibility,* then we should still strive to attain it, to seek it as far as possible. Although I may now hold a wide range of values and seem likely to employ them in the future, this fact by itself in no way precludes me from doing my best to eliminate them whenever and wherever I can." While we may strongly disagree with the position that our discipline is only obliged to produce knowledge, we may be able to demonstrate the need for a high-level, extraepistemic value orientation without introducing the issue of knowledge utilization. That is, we may accept the value-free adherent's reasoning above (provided he does not go on to argue that, as a result, the value-free position is *sufficient* for guiding our actions). In particular, we may agree that as individual sociologists employ

---

and innumerable new compounds. The biologist produces new hybrids, new genetic arrangements, and may shortly begin to intervene in genetic evolution on a massive scale. Our knowledge of ecology is likely to change the whole ecological system of the earth.

Social sciences are dominated by the fact that the social scientist and the knowledge he creates are themselves integral parts of the system which is being studied. Hence, the system changes as it is studied and because it is studied [Boulding, 1967, p. 12].

While not all such changes are foreseeable or significant, many are, and the question of their value remains. Further, responsibility for these changes can only be placed with the scientist who produces them.

extraepistemic value judgments (either because they feel that they ought to, or in the case of the value-free sociologists, because they do despite efforts to avoid them), a goal orientation must be chosen to help determine the values employed if we maintain any of the following:

1. We wish to avoid the hypocrisy of saying we are free from all values other than the value of knowledge when we are not; or
2. we feel that we must justify specific value choices that we *do* make by reference to a more general value orientation; or
3. we feel we have an obligation to evaluate the decisions made by other sociologists that have an impact extending beyond the discipline.

If the above points are accepted, and they will be here, both individual sociologists and the discipline as a whole must choose an extraepistemic goal orientation that could be used to guide, justify, and evaluate those values that *are* employed despite the efforts of some to avoid them.

Again, where extraepistemic values do play an important role in the discipline of sociology, the value-free position is both descriptively and prescriptively inadequate in dealing with them. As a result, it is argued that sociology must choose an extraepistemic value orientation. But which orientation should be chosen? Before turning to this question, let us briefly examine three major positions concerning values in sociology to see if they can help us answer it. Each position has numerous proponents and is initially quite attractive.

Sociology as Value Full—Value Explication

Occasionally one hears sociology students and faculty in conversation say that sociology must be "value full." Unfortunately, the meaning of this term is not quite clear. Presumably, it means that one should accept all values as legitimate (or why strive to be full of them?), yet the call for value fullness is usually preceded by a critical remark concerning the value of the activities that value-free sociologists are believed to engage in. A variant is that since sociologists cannot be value free, they must therefore be value full. If we take the phrase at face value this argument is analogous to "I cannot avoid eating and still live; therefore, I must make a pig of myself." Presumably, however, we do not have to incorporate all extraepistemic values into sociology—especially not those that are obviously contradictory or are simply not valued by anyone. Thus, the real meaning of value full probably is that sociology ought to be value relevant rather than value laden. However, saying that we should be value full in this sense is of as little help in making the choices we face as saying that we ought to be value free.

Related to the value-full position, and with similar problems, is the commonly held idea that since we cannot be value free we should clearly explicate the values that we employ in doing sociology (for example, see Braude, 1964, p. 399). Thus, because value judgments are unavoidable "there is and can be no value free sociology. The only choice is between an expression of one's values, as open and honest as it can be, this side of the psychoanalytical couch, and a vain ritual of moral neutrality which, because it invites men to ignore the vulnerability of reason to bias, leaves it at the mercy of irrationality" (Gouldner, 1962, p. 212).

We might at least expect that those who urge us to express our values should express their own, which is often not the case.* (It should be noted that saying some form of "I value that which is good" hardly constitutes an explication of one's values, since all it does is state that one has them.) More importantly, while all that seems required is for sociologists to express their values, this is hardly sufficient. One must agree that those who call for sociologists to express their values would not be entirely satisfied if all sociologists were to purchase soapboxes, stand upon them, and proudly proclaim all of their values. One might even suspect that when others often ask for values to be expressed, they do so because they have already guessed what the values are and wish to have them verbalized so that they may attack them more readily. At any rate,

* It should be pointed out that at least in a later article Gouldner (1968) does explicate his dominant value (which will be discussed in the final chapter).

all values are not equally valued by sociologists, any more than they are by others. While expressing values may be an important first step, it is not much help in choosing between them; nor does merely expressing values guarantee that their potential biasing effects will be eliminated.

The Ultimate Benefit of Knowledge

At the close of Chapter One, the idea of knowledge as an end in itself was discussed as a corollary of the value-free position. It was pointed out that this idea was usually put forth in conjunction with the notion that knowledge will ultimately be of benefit to mankind. Merton (1963, p. 86) contends that both an intrinsic and an ultimate rationale underlies all science. It is quite understandable that sociologists who by training and inclination come to love and revere knowledge would also hold the faith commitment that something that is believed to be good in itself will lead to a greater good. Since the goodness that is assumed to be brought about by knowledge is in the distant future, what clearly is involved *is* a faith commitment, or a hope.

This hope for ultimate usefulness and benefit is stated in different ways. Bendix states that "there is the hope that in the long run the constructive use of knowledge will prevail" (1970, p. 833). Sociologists do not go "so far as the famous mathematician who, when asked what he was doing, replied that whatever it was he hoped it would never be of use to anybody," but are willing to endure the "considerable time lag between their discovery and their final impression upon society" (Bierstedt, 1948, p. 316). Coser (1969, p. 132) states this faith commitment as well as anyone: "This [sociological enterprise], as all scientific enterprise, is ultimately grounded in the hope that greater knowledge of man will enhance his stature. While we may no longer be able to harbor the idea of the Enlightenment that the truth necessarily will set man free, we still cling obstinately to the hope that our endeavors will enhance the self-awareness of mankind and enable us, through self-conscious planning, to overcome at least some of the impediments that have been the burden of previous history."

The faith commitment that sociological knowledge will ultimately be beneficial is both attractive and comforting. Regrettably, it is not without difficulties. The first problem is that such statements of faith are unarguable. That is, once one sociologist states that "I have faith that sociological knowledge will ultimately issue a wide range of benefits to mankind," and a second states that "I have just as much faith that sociological knowledge will ultimately be harmful to mankind and eventually destroy it," they really can have very little more to say to one another on the topic. If the basis for their positions is merely faith, there is really no way of choosing between them. Still, if we treat the statement "Knowledge will ultimately be beneficial" as an assumption rather than a matter of faith, we can question its validity.

Lynd (1948, p. 2) contends that this faith in ultimate benefit originated in nineteenth-century optimism: "Immediate relevance has not been regarded as so important as ultimate relevance, and, in the burgeoning nineteenth century world which viewed all times as moving within the Master System of Progress, there was seemingly large justification for this optimistic tolerance. Our contemporary world is losing its confidence in the inevitability of Progress. Men's ways of ordering their common lives have broken down so disastrously as to make hope precarious."

Assuming that no master plan will lead to the beneficent use of knowledge, there is no reason to assume that men will use knowledge to the benefit of mankind. Further, as discussed earlier, if knowledge is ethically neutral in that it can be used for a wide variety of ends, both beneficial and harmful, then it seems unwarranted to assume that knowledge will lead to ultimate benefit.

In the final analysis, it is probably impossible to predict whether knowledge is of ultimate benefit, especially since there are innumerable conceptions of what is beneficial. Holding such a general faith commitment creates a dilemma. If it is left at such a general level, there is no way of knowing the likelihood that "ultimate benefit" will be achieved or whether the conception of what is beneficial held by one person is congruent or antithetical to the conception held by others. On the other hand, if the benefit is specified, it is likely that many will disagree on its goodness. Further, even if the nature of the benefit is agreed on, the question remains, Are the odds so good that this benefit will occur without active intervention that we should risk not attaining it? If it is a benefit, why should we not seek it directly rather than merely hope for its occurrence?

Finally, the hope that knowledge will ultimately be beneficial does not, due to its lack of specificity, help us in choosing values to employ in doing sociology. Saying that sociological knowledge will ultimately be beneficial does not indicate that one is neutral with regard to values, but only that one is unable or unwilling to specify them. At the same time, it is of little help in guiding value choices, as is the position of value freedom.

Sociological Relevance

In addition to those who see an ultimate benefit of sociology, there are also those who seek an immediate benefit. Lynd (1948), while claiming that in social science "immediate relevance has not been regarded as so important as ultimate relevance" (p. 2), argues that immediate relevance should be given priority and that research and activities of social scientists should be made relevant to the problems of the day.

Some argue that while it is quite permissible for the sociologist to do pure research, it should be made relevant, "after an appraisal that may well be agonizing, [by] declaring all the social consequences he [the sociologist] may foresee, however dimly, which are even remotely likely to follow the disclosure not only of his own contributions to science but also those of other scientists within his wide area of competence" (R. Watson-Watt, in Bennis, 1968, p. 253). Others argue that immediate relevance of research must be weighted more heavily.

Preceding research, the extent to which various possible investigations would contribute to the body of sociological theory and the solution of social problems should be appraised. Since both may not be maximized in any single piece of research, it is suggested that relevance to social problems must be maximized. Beal (1969, pp. 473–474) argues in this way for optimizing sociological relevance: "Basically what I have argued for is that it is probable that the maximization of the goals of conceptual development, theory building and testing, measurement, improvement in analysis techniques, and research on significant social problems are at some point in conflict. With the present state of knowledge, methodology, personnel, and funds, we cannot maximize all of these goals. . . . I am . . . arguing for a heavier weighting of the contribution of the knowledge produced to the relevant social problems variable in the optimizing model."

Still others argue that it is not sufficient for the knowledge of a social science to be relevant—the lives of social scientists themselves must be directed towards relevant action. Thus, Bennis offers a general plea for relevant social activity: "I see no alternative to an active role for the Faculties of Social Sciences. This means they should not only adapt to societies, but that they should also influence society directly" (1968, p. 252). Similarly, Etzkowitz argues, "As sociologists we do not have to confine ourselves to merely understanding and analyzing what others are doing. As sociologists, we have the possibility, as well as the moral obligation, to enter into the institutional life of our society to initiate reforms or even to take part in the construction of new institutional conceptions as social realities" (1969, p. 12).

It should be noted that pleas for relevance in sociology are met with criticism, and some of these criticisms have already been encountered in terms of the value-free and knowledge for its own sake positions. One primary criticism is that emphasizing relevance may have a dilatory effect on the body of sociological knowledge. Thus, on the one hand, Coser states that while the work of scientists such as Freud and Mendel seemed irrelevant at the time, their work had a profound and revolutionary impact on the world as well as on the body of knowledge. On the other hand, "the majority of those men who, in their day, worked on the 'relevant issues' remain of interest, at best, to specialized historians of ideas" (Coser, 1969, p. 132). Contrary to Coser, it may be argued that it was precisely those who worked on the "relevant issues" of their day, such as Pasteur, who significantly contributed to their respective sciences. This may be especially true of sociology if Kultgen is correct when he argues that there is a close relationship between sociological and social problems: "It is no accident, however, that problems are so often socially and sociologically important. In society humans are doing what in sociology humans are studying. . . . What large numbers of people identify as serious social problems are likely to involve basic and disputed questions about the relation of man to his social environment" (1970, pp. 183–184). Yet the question of the actual historical impact which knowledge that was sought for its direct relevance has had on the bodies of knowledge is difficult to assess. Since numerous examples and counterexamples could be mustered for each side of the issue, the question of the contribution of relevant research to the body of knowledge through the history of science is probably best left to those best qualified—the historians of science.

A more telling criticism of the pleas for relevance may be that they are hollow or empty. This is so in two senses: First, sociologists are already relevant, and second, these pleas do not tell us to what we should be relevant.

It must be pointed out that those sociologists who would presumably be the objects of the accusations of irrelevancy are often doing research that is relevant to the body of sociological knowledge. However, it may be argued by those who make such pleas that "this criticism is unfair. Clearly by the term *relevant* we mean relevant to valued ends that are nonepistemic in nature." Even though it may not be clear to us what the nature of the requested relevance is, we may grant this, and still the criticism that the pleas are hollow stands. This is because sociologists are also doing, and have been doing, research that is relevant to nonepistemic valued ends as well.

> Also, it must be stressed that, to a considerable degree, sociologists are engaged in studies that *are* relevant, and which usually involve a value judgment even if it is unstated. What else are we to make of all the studies on crime, delinquency, race relations, the family, industrial sociology, suicide, urban problems and political behavior and so on?
>
> Few people will argue that the issues . . . are not relevant, and it seems fairly clear that most of the sociologists involved are against crime, delinquency, and suicide, and are concerned with understanding these phenomena in order to help in their prevention and control. In fact, these judgments are often quite explicitly stated [Biblarz, 1969, p. 3].

Sociologists, then, are and have been relevant. While they recognize the relevance of sociology, there are those who strongly oppose the ways in which relevance is manifested.

> In at least one sense, there seems to be little doubt about the *relevance* of the discipline as presently constituted. . . . As consultants, managers, and administrators, sociologists have had the sense of being centrally involved in policy formation and implementation. Involvement and relevance have been manifested in as many ways as policy and fashion dictated: one generation of social scientists would provide the social science brief for discriminatory immigration laws; the next would as assuredly document the case for school desegregation. And with the rise of national welfare bureaucracies, the proliferation of private and public funding agencies, and the adaptation of the university to governmental needs, the sociologist has clearer evidence for believing in his *relevance*—but all too often fails to recognize that his prime relevance is to a limited category of political, corporate, and bureaucratic clients [Colfax, 1970, p. 73].

Whether or not we hold the values to which sociology is currently directed, it must be recognized that sociology is in fact relevant to some values.* Much of this chapter supports the idea that the call for relevance is hollow by demonstrating that sociologists are seeking knowledge which is usable by themselves and others for valued ends and that they are directly involved in attaining such ends. There are innumerable examples in the past and the present of sociology being made relevant to a wide range of social concerns. These include areas such as law enforcement, the development of foreign policy, race relations, social planning with regard to poverty, coping with aging, community development, manpower, public health, peace research, and adaptation to rapid change (for

---

* It is difficult to explain why these calls for relevance persist, but it may be that the concept of relevance may be used egocentrically. In other words, research is accused of irrelevance if it is irrelevant to those ends which the accuser values.

detailed examples of sociological relevance in these and other areas, see Lazarsfeld, Sewell, and Wilensky, 1967; Shostak, 1974).

These pleas for relevance are hollow in a second sense—they do not tell us to what we should be relevant. As a result they are of little help in guiding the choices we must make. For example, consider how much the following exhortation actually tells us: "It is much simpler to withdraw from the world of men and rather contemplate them from the Olympian heights of abstruse scholarship. It is precisely this which the sociologist has done. He has surrendered to an image of science his mandate not only to discover but to *use* his knowledge for the human weal. It is not enough to say as he has said: I have knowledge; here it is to use—by others. It is not enough to retire from the field, *hors de combat*. The sociologist has the responsibility to enter the fray and, as sociologist, cry out for a better human condition than now obtains" (Braude, 1964, p. 398).

While some find exhortations such as these uplifting and exhilarating, in the final analysis they tell us very little. "A better human condition" is desirable, but just what might it be? We often have little idea about what ends sociologists should value and to what their research activity should be relevant. To say that the work of sociologists should be relevant to social problems says little more than that we should not value what should not be valued. In other words, these pleas merely urge us to seek the good and avoid the bad, but leave unanswered the question as to what each of these are. Some of these pleas for relevance are more specific about the social problems to which they refer—war, crime, poverty, for example. However, still left unspecified are the values that underlie these choices and the justification for those values.

> Thus Robert Lynd, in *Knowledge for What?*, contrasted the gravity of our social problems with the triviality of much social research. "Seismologists watching a volcano" he called the fact finders, and he appealed to them to tackle manfully their main job, which is to reconstruct our whole society. Max Lerner enthusiastically applauded this "unashamed instrumentalism." He hailed Lynd for having staked out "the most spa-

cious claims for the possibilities of social thinking"; he condemned the "detachment" and "objectivity" of other social scientists as mere "dodges to avoid thinking, devices for saving their skins." Both men are saying, at bottom, that now is the time for all good men to come to the aid of their country [Muller, 1964, p. 174].

Unfortunately, these and similar pleas offer little more in terms of the nature and justification of the values to which sociology should be relevant. As Muller adds, "Unhappily, these stirring words do not solve the actual problem (not to mention the question of just what a scientist can *do* about a volcano)" (1964, p. 174). In short, these pleas do not allow us the means for making the necessary value choices. Early in this chapter the value-free position was criticized for not helping us to deal with the extraepistemic values that are present in sociology and seem likely to continue in the future. We have further seen that sociological relevance, as well as the value-full explication and the knowledge as ultimate value positions are similarly unhelpful in dealing with extraepistemic values, even though analysis of these issues makes us all the more aware that values are present and must be dealt with. This is not to say that each of these positions has not performed a valuable and necessary service—they have, but it is now time to go beyond them.

As Benne (1965) points out, the fact that there is so much concern about values by sociologists and other social scientists is rather unusual. It would not be surprising, under conditions where power is unequally distributed, for those who possess the predominance of power to discuss the validity and value of their possessing that power, or for those with relatively little power to attempt to sanction the norms that restrict the exercise of control by those in power. "It is probably more unusual for men with some new legacy of power to seek norms controlling their own exercise of that power in their relations with others" (Benne, 1965, p. 1). Social scientists now have some limited power, "and accumulating behavioral knowledge promises to enlarge the power of psychologists and other behavioral scientists over others. What normative orientation, what value system, should constrain and guide the scientist in the exercise of and contribution to behavioral control?" (p. 1).

The question of what normative orientation sociology as a profession and sociologists as individuals should choose must now be met squarely. It is finally time to actually explicate our values and cease calling for their explication. We must deal with the questions of what benefit sociology is likely to be in the future and to what valued ends it should be relevant.

It has been argued in the preceding pages that sociologists face numerous decisions that cannot be made solely by referring to pure knowledge concerns. Further, the profession as a whole needs an extraepistemic reference with which to evaluate these decisions. What must now be discussed and debated is the decision orientation or goal orientation that can serve as such a point of reference. Also, both individual sociologists and the profession as a whole are faced with questions concerning how sociologists might justifiably use the knowledge themselves, and what uses of sociological knowledge by others should be encouraged or discouraged. The answers to these questions again require a decision orientation and a specification of the ends we are seeking in terms of a goal orientation.*

The choice of a decision or goal orientation demands a discussion of its justification. Chapter Four presents a discussion of the skeptic's view concerning the use of facts as the basis for the choice of a nonepistemic orientation. Chapter Six returns to the question of the basis for choosing an orientation, discussing an evolutionary-naturalistic view, which clearly runs counter to the skeptic's view.

---

* Since the setting of a high-level goal orientation provides a reference for evaluating decisions, and one high-level orientation can suggest both subgoals and decisions as to how to obtain the subgoals, the terms *decision orientation* and *goal orientation* are used interchangeably, although they may be conceived in other contexts as analytically distinct.

Three

The Skeptic's View
of Facts and Values

Sociologists are now in a position where they must explicitly discuss extraepistemic decision orientations which may direct choices involved in seeking knowledge, the action by sociologists, and the use of sociological knowledge. If we consider a value to be a standard of worth that expresses a preference (Kaplan, 1964, p. 370), a system of values may then be considered as a system of preferences. Boulding (1967, p. 12–13) argues that any subculture holds a system of value preferences that distinguishes the subculture from other subcultures. More importantly, each subculture possesses a metavalue or set of metavalues, which Boulding terms an *ethic* (and that is termed here a *decision orientation* or *goal orientation*), that can be used "for evaluating and legitimating preference systems" (Boulding, 1967, p. 12). Science may similarly be said to be a subculture with its own established and explicit decision orientation. As

Boulding points out, this orientation exists in two closely related yet distinguishable forms: "There is, in the first place, a high preference for veracity. The only really unforgivable sin of the scientist is deliberate deception and the publication of false results. The career of any scientist who has destroyed his credibility in this way is virtually over. . . . Along with the preference for veracity goes a strong preference for truth. These are not the same things. Veracity is the absence of deceit, and truth is the absence of error" (1967, p. 13).

This set of metavalues or orientation of science, including sociology, is clearly epistemic in nature and allows evaluation of a large number of lower-level value systems. On the basis of the preceding chapters, it may be argued that a similar, nonepistemic orientation is needed in sociology. This would allow evaluation and legitimation of lower-level value systems inherent in making the necessary choices involved in seeking and using sociological knowledge that cannot be made solely on the basis of knowledge-related values. Ideally, we would like to prove the validity of our choice of an orientation. However, this may not be possible.

There are those who argue that the correctness of values may be proven by empirical testing. In other words, the correctness of values exists to be discovered and may therefore be considered objective.* Thus, Kolb points out that there is a group of sociologists who believe that "somehow in the structure of the universe values objectively exist independently of their apprehension and espousal by man. Thus if it is objectively wrong to commit murder it is wrong even though no man knows or no man espouses it" (in Dewey and Humber, 1966, p. 647). Since values inhere in objects, their correctness may be proven or discovered empirically. For example, a sociologist can prove that a certain social arrangement is wrong because it leads to hunger. Therefore, sociologists can presumably study the social world and discover which nonepistemic orientation should guide their discipline.

---

* The idea that values may be treated as objective is argued in a different way by those who hold what philosophers term the *intuitionist* perspective (which states, in part, that human beings possess a unique faculty for intuiting values, that value statements are therefore descriptive statements, and that values are objective but unobservable).

A contrary position to this is offered here. We call it the "skeptic's view," in that it is skeptical about our ability to validate or justify claims of value solely by referring to knowledge claims or facts. According to the skeptic's view, the idea that the correctness of values is empirically provable is undemonstrated. Ultimately, the skeptic's view asserts that the validity of values *cannot* be demonstrated by referring to facts. This assertion is based on the idea that every statement of value is based on a prior, higher-level value judgment. Each statement of value at increasingly higher levels in turn demands yet a higher-level value judgment until finally a metavalue is chosen that is merely asserted or assumed to be of value.* In short, the justification of every value requires higher level values until we reach a value whose worth is necessarily assumed.

Consider the case of an agricultural reform in a culture. How is a sociologist to determine that this reform is of value? After studying the reform he says, "I have discovered that this reform is not to be valued because it leads to unproductively sized farm plots." When asked why unproductively sized farm plots are not valuable, he responds that "they lead to low crop yields." When asked why low crop yields are not to be valued, he refers to numerous other valued states until he finally says "because it leads to hunger." As strongly as many of us hold this higher-level negative value of hunger, the adherent to the skeptic's view would argue that it must be recognized that hunger's lack of value is also assumed and that there are groups that value hunger, offer rationales to support it, and under certain circumstances are willing to fast until death. In testing any particular value, the point at which a higher-level value must be assumed will, of course, vary.

Often a question of value will regress to a question of the value of existence. Consider the case of a particular tree. According to the skeptic's view, there is no way for us to *see* value in the tree.

---

* It should be pointed out that the skeptic's view does not contradict the idea that *in practice* the values of groups change with changes in the conception of facts, or that the choice of values may be explainable sociologically in terms of fact. Rather, this view argues that values themselves cannot be validated or justified solely by referring to facts. In short, the skeptic's view sees an important separation between explaining held values and justifying them. In Chapter Six a contrary evolutionary-naturalistic view is presented that strongly challenges this separation.

This is because there is no value inherent in it, but rather the value is imposed by us.* In contrast, it may be argued that we do not see the value of the tree because values do not exist in objects or states of affairs but rather in relations between them. The skeptic may grant this and ask that we relate the tree to other things around it. We find that the tree is of value to the bird who uses it for a nest, to the house builder who needs wood, or to the hill which it prevents erosion of. All of these statements of value relations assume that the bird, the house builder, and the hill are themselves of value, and the tree gains value by contributing to their welfare. We may look to still other relations to support the contention that the bird, house builder, and hill are valuable. Ultimately, however, we must reach a point where we arbitrarily say that the existence of X (for example, the house builder) is of value. But what warrants the statement that the existence of X is of value?

Without referring to another value, it cannot be demonstrated that the existence of X is of greater value than the existence of Y, in that existence must equal existence. More telling still, it is not possible to demonstrate that the existence of X is of greater value than the nonexistence of X. If this were the case, all that is ought to be. As logically odd as it might appear, we can say further that nonexistence is just another form of existence (in that as far as we know matter and energy do not cease to exist but rather change form and are continually reorganizing). More concretely, would the universe be of less value if man had never existed in it?† Ultimately, according to the skeptic's view, we must assume even the value of a given existence—its value is neither discoverable nor demonstrable (unless, of course, we refer to some assumed higher-level value). It is asserted then that the validity of values is not

---

* It is important to note that while it is argued that values do not inhere in the object, this in no way denies that valuing is an interactive process. That is, there must exist an object to value as well as a valuer for valuing to take place. Yet this interactional process of valuing is primarily one of imposing value on the valued object by the valuer.

† All that would be lost, perhaps, are values themselves. Parenthetically, it can be argued that mankind has added value to the universe because he can comprehend it, and if man had never existed this possibility and thus value would be lost. While this idea may be comforting to man, it is unclear how this would benefit the universe, or how the universe would be of less value for never having been comprehended.

demonstrable or provable by referring to facts, since such a demonstration rests upon an a priori assumption of value.

A refutation to the skeptic's view is that the value of some states of affairs is discoverable, since certain high-level values are shared by all mankind; therefore, we can determine whether a state of affairs is to be valued by seeing if it concurs with these universally shared values. Similarly, some lower-level values can be said to be consistent or inconsistent with higher-level values. Even granting these points, it is unlikely that any universally held highest-level value exists. Even if such a value was found, its value would only be universally assumed; it would not necessarily be valid because it is universally held.

Whether there are in fact any universally held high-level values probably can be empirically tested if we are willing to commit the immense time and resources necessary. However, as stated above, even if such a test was carried out, it seems highly unlikely that it would yield a universally held highest-level value. For example, consider the possibility of all men valuing their own existence. While there would be those who do prefer life over any other value, there would also be those who prefer nonexistence over certain forms of existence. In short, there are those who would prefer death to life.

In the same vein, while societies probably consider a person who commits suicide to be irrational, there is no necessary reason for sociologists to make the same characterization. Clearly all of us can imagine how one could quite reasonably choose to commit suicide rather than continue in that form of existence. No matter how strongly we may disagree with their actions, it is likely that *we* are being irrational if we assume that every kamikaze pilot in World War II was irrational.*

As is the case with existence, there seems to be no highest-

* It is unclear if there have been any societies that, when faced with what appeared to be intolerable circumstances, chose nonexistence directly or courses of action that were recognized as likely to lead to nonexistence. At any rate, one can clearly conceive of such a choice (if societies can make choices), and certainly there are numerous examples of societies going to war in which they risked nonexistence for the sake of other valued ends, suggesting that societal existence was not the highest value.

level value that is held universally. It is important to note that even if there were such a universally held value, no validity would be conferred upon it just because it is universally valued; we would only have discovered a value that is universally assumed.

In sum, then, the skeptic's view asserts that values are ultimately not demonstrable by referring to facts. As such, this view can probably best be categorized by what is termed in the philosophical literature a *noncognitivist* or *nondescriptivist* view. As Frankena points out, "The most extreme of these are a number of views that deny ethical judgments, or at least the most basic ones, to be capable of any kind of rational or objectively valid justification" (1973, p. 105). The skeptic's view clearly would concur with such a position. Strictly speaking, however, it seems that philosophers assume that noncognitivist theories address not only the undemonstrability of values, but also the nature of the meaning of value statements. For example, emotivists argue that value statements, rather than making a statement of fact, actually express deep-seated emotions. To illustrate, one emotivist, A. J. Ayer, "has suggested that ethical predicates are like exclamation points of a special kind, that 'Stealing is wrong!' is a misleading way of putting 'Stealing!!!' where the triple exclamation point is taken to express horror or indignation" (Brandt, 1959, p. 204). Some logical positivists, like Rudolf Carnap, agree that value statements do not describe anything, but consider them to be disguised commands. Thus, Carnap would interpret "Stealing is wrong!" to mean "Do not steal." Both Carnap and Ayer would agree that value sentences are forms of speech that are important to social life, but they certainly do not state facts or describe what is true or false (Brandt, 1959, p. 204). Still other views on the meaning of ethical statements have been offered, such as that of Bertrand Russell, who held that moral judgments merely express a kind of wish (Frankena, 1973, p. 105). In presenting the skeptic's view, no specific theory of the meaning of ethical statements has been offered, and presenting such a theory seems unnecessary for present purposes. However, at a general level the various theories seem to concur that value statements are nondescriptive and nonfactual, even though they sometimes may be improperly presented as the contrary. Thus, the skeptic's view seems most appropriately classified philosophically with the noncognitivists or nondescriptivists, even though its prime focus is the justification, rather than the closely related area of the meaning, of value statements.

In the preceding pages, the skeptic's view of the relationship between facts and values has been presented. It asserts that the validity or correctness of values is ultimately not demonstrable by referring to facts—in short, unless a high-level value is simply assumed, one cannot legitimately go from an "is" to an "ought." At the same time, the values held by individuals, groups, and societies can be explained by the social sciences without referring to a mystical or cosmic source from which all values were once universally believed to have sprung. It may be implied that if the skeptic's view is adopted and values are not seen as validated by facts or the allowance of a mystical origin, values have been robbed of their importance. Yet that need not follow, for even if the social sciences reach the point where the holding of values is fully explained, values would remain important to humanity, since it acts on the basis of them (even if we rename or reconceptualize them). When we explain something, we merely explain it—we do not explain it away. Muller (1964, p. 33) argues cogently in this area:

> And the familiar statement that human life is "meaningless" may itself be meaningless for practical purposes. All readers are acquainted with the melancholy picture: of matter as a mad dance of electrons, of life as "a disease which afflicts matter in its old age," of man as a forked form of life that has learned to strut and fret—of the whole witless show playing itself out mechanically before an empty house, the only issue being whether the universe is exploding or running down. But in denying the existence of a consciousness outside the universe, an intelligible purpose behind the whole enterprise, the disenchanted forget that there is nevertheless a consciousness aware of the universe, and that life has a very urgent meaning for those who consciously live it. If man's purposes make little perceptible difference to the universe, they make a great deal to him.
>
> Yet neither is this to say that whatever is is right. We cannot prove that it is better to be a human

being dissatisfied than a pig satisfied, even if we alone
know both sides of the question. We cannot say that
consciousness and thought must be good because nature
produced them; nature has produced, and destroyed,
all kinds of oddities.

When we explain why someone finds a situation meaningful, with
all the necessary references to socialization, reinforcement contin-
gencies, environmental constraints, or what have you, we make the
situation no less meaningful to that person. Nor have we demonstrated that it is invalid to find it meaningful.

Even when a child cries over something that we consider
insignificant, we need not deny the reality of the hurt or pronounce
it insignificant to the child. Similarly, while it makes no assumption
concerning the existence of God and assumes that religious beliefs
are explainable, the sociology of religion does not assume that religious practices are insignificant or that the feelings that lead to
them are not deep. In short, neither assuming that the possession of
values is explainable in natural terms nor asserting with the skeptic
that the validity of values is undemonstrable implies that values are
or should be insignificant in human life.

Moreover, the assertion that the validity of values is ultimately not demonstrable or provable by referring to facts goes no
farther. It does not assert that all values are ultimately invalid.
They may in fact be valid, but there is simply no way of demonstrating their validity. Just as the sociology of religion assumes that
the existence of God is not demonstrable without affirming or denying His existence, so the skeptic argues that the validity of values
is undemonstrable without affirming or denying their ultimate
validity.

Also, the skeptic's view does not necessarily imply an extreme
form of ethical relativism. Presumably one who accepts ethical
relativism would argue that *all* individual (or group, or societal)
value stances are *valid* relative to each individual (or group, or
society). To the contrary, the skeptic would argue that in the final
analysis all such stances are of nondemonstrable, assumed validity;
all values are not equally valid, but rather they are equally *non-
demonstrable*. What is argued, then, is not some form of extreme
relativism, but a form of extreme skepticism.

Since it is held that the validity of all values is equally non-demonstrable, knowing the characteristics of a social unit that holds a particular set of values does not make the values more demonstrable. Thus, a corollary of the skeptic's view may be offered: No characteristics of a social unit holding certain values confer any extra, special validity on those values. In this limited sense, it is asserted that no individual's values are of greater validity than those of any other individual due to their own personal characteristics. For example, an individual's values are not of greater validity because she holds a position of authority in a religious community and makes claim of divine inspiration. Although certain individuals are better able to convince others to adopt their own values or to actualize goals inspired by those values due to greater power, access to resources, or ingenuity, this does not confer any greater validity on their values.

This implies that the values of sociologists are no more valid than anyone else's. This is not implied by the counterassertion, discussed earlier, that the correctness of values is discoverable. If the correctness of values is discoverable empirically and thus is closely related to facts, the sociologist should have the correct conception of the "good society," since he knows the most about social life. His knowledge would allow him to make correct value judgments; his empirical competence would imply a competence in making value judgments. "It [the doctrine of value freedom] is inappropriate—for if the discipline which claims to know the most about the nature of social life does not offer its most reasoned judgments, to whom does the obligation fall? It would seem to those less competent to make them—which also seems absurd" (Gray, 1968, p. 180). This statement confuses epistemic competence with competence in making value judgments. The validity of the values of sociologists has no less an assumptive basis than the validity of any other people's values. If sociological knowledge determines the correctness of values and dictates action, presumably we should administer a test of sociological knowledge—perhaps the advanced Graduate Record Examination in sociology might do. Find the sociologist who scores highest and say, "Tell us what we should value and tell us what we should do." However, even if the skeptic admits that this sociologist can best show us the means to actualize our values or show us the implications of them, there is no reason for assuming that the sociologist's values are ultimately more valid. On this point, the skeptic's view probably agrees with the value-free position that "the scientific method as such provides no technique for answering questions of value, for determining ultimate ends" (Bierstedt, 1948, p. 312), and thus scientists have no monopoly on "correct" values.

Gouldner attempts to place us on the horns of a dilemma in this matter. We have just discussed the first horn—that of technical competence. "If technical competence does provide a warrant for making value judgments there is nothing to prohibit sociologists from making them within the area of their expertise. If, on the contrary, technical competence provides no warrant for making value judgments, then at least sociologists are as free to do so as anyone else; then their value judgments are at least as good as anyone else's, say a twelve year old child's" (1962, p. 200).

The second horn of this dilemma is not really problematic if we take Gouldner at face value. Sociologists are *just* as free as anyone else to make value judgments, and those value judgments have ultimately the *same* validity as anyone else's. Clearly, then, the sociologist by virtue of being a sociologist has no right to dictate the values of others. Sociologists, it is argued, can no more than others discover the correctness of values, and claims of greater knowledge or intelligence make values no more correct.

The skeptic's view as presented would not, of course, be without critics. An alternate view will be presented in Chapter Five that offers a very different position at several points. This work does not attempt or demand a choice between the two views. Rather, it is suggested that both positions are sufficiently persuasive for many sociologists to accept some form of either. As such, it seems worthwhile to examine the implications of adopting either view for choosing a goal orientation by the discipline of sociology.

If the skeptic's view is accepted, sociology is seemingly placed in an irreconcilably difficult position. On one hand, nonepistemic values significantly enter at numerous points in the knowledge-gathering process and shape the resulting body of knowledge, as well as decisions concerning its use by sociologists and nonsociologists alike. It was argued in the preceding chapter that we need to choose an orientation to guide the value choices involved in sociology. On the other hand, the validity of such a value orientation is ultimately assumptive, and sociologists cannot demonstrate the greater validity of one orientation over another by reference to facts.* Thus, we are placed in the awkward position of having to choose with no adequate grounds for doing so.

---

* The type of reasoning that has led to this statement has probably led some to feel that value freedom is the only tenable position. However, this would only be the case if the arguments in the preceding chapter—that sociology is, and most likely will continue to be, not value free, and thus we must choose—are not accepted. In sum, the reasoning presented suggests that while we must choose, the grounds for our choice are not as absolute as would ideally be the case.

Four

CCCCCCCCCCCCCCCCCCCCCCCCCCC

A Proposed Orientation for the Profession

ༀༀༀༀༀༀༀༀༀༀༀༀༀༀༀༀༀༀༀༀༀༀༀༀༀ

If the preceding analysis of the skeptic's view is accepted, we are faced with what seems to be an insoluble dilemma. The profession must choose an extraepistemic orientation in order to make the necessary evaluations of the numerous possibilities in seeking and employing sociological knowledge. At the same time we recognize that any orientation that is chosen cannot be proven "correct" and that its validity is ultimately assumed. This apparent dilemma can, however, be resolved.

The skeptic's view does not imply that the choice of an orientation is impossible, but only that the ultimate value of the orientation cannot be demonstrated and is only assumptive; thus, the best we can do in arguing for an orientation is to offer persuasive reasons. Since any orientation for guiding the search for and the employment of sociological knowledge has implications for either maintaining or changing elements in the social structure that may or may not be valued by those who participate in society, it at least indirectly imposes values on the societal members. While Chapter Two argued that a choice of orientation is necessary, Chapter Three argued that sociologists have no warrant for imposing values as a result of characteristics possessed by them, whether it be greater intelligence, knowledge, or power. However, there is one orientation that might be adopted by the profession that can uniquely aid decision making while minimizing unwarranted value imposition: the seeking of societies which embody social structures that optimize alternatives (or freedom) for their members.* Given the preceding discussion, it is recognized at the outset that the value of the orientation is assumptive rather than demonstrable. As a result, we partly agree with the psychologist Kelman, who, while suggesting that freedom is an essential part of being human, implicitly acknowledges that this value is assumptively based.

> The purpose of education and of the arrangement of the social order, as I see it, is to enable men to live in society while at the same time enhancing their freedom of choice and widening their areas of choice. I recognize as ethically ambiguous any action that limits freedom of choice, whether it be through punishment or reward or even through so perfect an arrangement of society that people do not care to choose. I cannot defend this value because it is not logically derived from anything else. I can, of course, offer supporting arguments for it. . . . While I can offer these supporting arguments, I recognize that freedom of choice is, in the final analysis, a rock-bottom value for me [1965, p. 35].

Although the validity of the proposed orientation is only assumed, it seems fair to demand that the reasons for adopting it be

---

* The term *freedom* here is used synonomously with the phrase *optimization of alternatives*, since many who use the term imply this. However, it is recognized that the term *freedom* is perilously used since it has other common usages that are clearly excluded later in this section, such as the meaning "absence of constraints."

persuasive. Given the difficulties presented by the skeptic's view, a particularly persuasive reason for adopting this orientation is that it uniquely mitigates those difficulties. In particular, this orientation, the optimization of the freedom of alternatives, avoids unwarranted imposition of sociologists' values upon the rest of the population.

To elaborate, we may say that freedom is optimized when alternatives or choices are optimized, whether these alternatives be in thought, speech, or action. More formally, it is urged that sociology adopt as its primary nonepistemic orientation: *the optimization of alternatives open to every individual.*

While less important reasons will be offered later, it is urged that this orientation be chosen because it has the prime virtue of allowing sociologists to make and evaluate value choices concerning the use of sociological knowledge, while minimizing value imposition upon the rest of the population. The effects of unwarranted value imposition are mitigated because the optimization of alternatives allows every individual, to the maximum degree possible, to act in accordance with her own values and actualize them in the form of goals. The goal of sociology, then, would not be to impose a specific conception of what is good upon others, but rather to seek a social structure or social structures that optimizes the alternatives open to every individual by which she can actualize her own conceptions of good.*

Any time sociological knowledge is used to change or maintain a social system, some form of manipulation or control must occur. Kelman suggests that this is also true about changes in individual behavior: "Effective behavior change inevitably involves

---

* It should be pointed out that the argument here may be considered paradoxical given the discussion in Chapter Three. In the skeptic's view ought statements cannot gain validity from statements of what is, and yet the optimizing orientation is said to be supported by the skeptic's view, which is itself a statement of what is at the broadest level. Even if it is assumed that an argument's being paradoxical is a significant criticism, (1) Chapter Three dealt with facts as a basis for demonstrating validity rather than as a basis for persuasive reasons, and (2) more importantly, an argument may be paradoxical in a trivial way; for instance, the paradox contained in the argument that "there are no absolutes" is paradoxical if it is stated in absolute terms, which seems necessary to make the argument, but the accusation does not have much bearing on the substance of the argument.

some degree of manipulation or control, and at least the implicit imposition of the change agent's values on the client or the person he is influencing" (1965, p. 33). In short, some type of intervention must be made to produce a desired state that would not occur if the system was left to its own devices. The orientation that minimizes the imposition of the values of the controller or manipulator and maximizes the values of the client or person being influenced is argued to be the optimization of alternatives open to every individual.

For comparison, consider an example of behavioral manipulation in accordance with the minimization of alternatives open to every individual.

There exists a wide range of alternative environments, both social and physical, open to every individual from which to choose. Further, an individual can choose from a wide range of alternative behavioral repertoires that correspond to particular environments. For example, let us consider a simplified presentation of recreational alternatives.

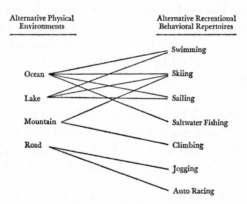

FIGURE 1. Mapped Physical Environments and Recreational Behavioral Repertoires.

In Figure 1 four alternative physical environments are presented in which recreational behavior might occur. Also listed are seven types of recreational activities or behavioral repertoires. Any recreational environment has a particular set of behaviors that is appropriate to it, while other sets are not. Similarly, any recreational repertoire is appropriate to certain environments and not to others. In this sense, the behavioral repertoires are "mapped" to the environments. That is, certain environments permit a certain range of behaviors, and the desire to behave in a certain way predisposes one to seek certain environments.

Now assume that a group of people place a negative value on skiing and have access to the knowledge and the resources necessary for manipulation. They could either prevent access to environments where skiing was possible, that is, oceans, lakes, or mountains, or they could eliminate the behavioral repertoire of skiing. Similarly, they could use the available knowledge and the consequent ability to manipulate and control to insure that positively valued recreation will occur by eliminating both the availability of other environments where that recreation does not occur and the other recreational behaviors that correspond to the remaining environments. In both cases, the impact of the manipulation is the minimization of open alternatives.

In general, the body of sociological knowledge can be used in this way to decrease alternatives. However, it can also be used for the purpose of expanding both the number of alternative social environments and the number of possible behaviors available to individuals within any given social or physical environment. Choosing to optimize the alternatives open to every individual is choosing to optimize the values of those who act (all), rather than only those who control (the few). The most basic choice of a sociological orientation is between optimizing alternatives open to every individual and increasing the choices and freedom of those who control while decreasing choice and freedom of those who act.

If the general minimization of alternatives is chosen, it makes very little difference who the manipulator is who places the actualization of his values above freedom of choice. Whether the sociologist provides the knowledge necessary for imposing values to politicians (in a decisionist model), or whether sociologists impose their own values by virtue of their professional qualifications (in a rationalist model; see Eisele, 1971–1972, p. 101), matters very little in terms of the extent to which freedom is removed. Whether the model is decisionist or rationalist, the imposition of values (especially from the point of view of the optimization orientation presented here) "is completely inadequate, since decisions about human existence are made by men who are not capable of deciding them. Decision-making is kept out of the public realm. The public can do no more than legitimize the power of decision-making elites" (Eisele, 1971–1972, p. 101). The orientation of the optimization of alternatives assumes that those best able and most justified to make decisions about human existence are those who live that existence. Thus, it optimizes the choices open to every individual, and thus freedom, rather than proposing that some select few possess values that are sufficiently justified to warrant abrogating that freedom.

Two Other Conceptions of Freedom

In addition to clarifying the orientation of optimization of freedom as the optimization of alternatives open to every individual by comparing it to its opposite, we may also contrast the optimization of freedom to two other conceptions of freedom.

In the expression *optimization of freedom,* the term *freedom* does not mean *freedom from constraint or limits.* Although the optimization of alternatives does decrease the limits placed on choice, society imposes limits on any individual's behavior—any social environment, even one that optimizes alternatives, constrains behavior as do physical environments. Freedom, then, is a social relationship, and not a lack of relationship. "Freedom emerges as a continual process of liberation, as a fight . . . to remain *dependent. . . .* Freedom is not a solipsistic existence but a sociological action. It is not a condition limited to the single individual but a relationship, even though it is a relationship from the standpoint of the individual" (Simmel, in Wolff, 1950, p. 120–121).

The society necessary to optimize alternatives open to every individual still structures and constrains behavior, in that although the range of alternatives is broadened, it is still limited. While increasing the number of alternatives makes the society increasingly complex, the structuring of alternatives allows an organized complexity of individual behaviors, and not the chaotic "everybody doing his own thing." To summarize this point, freedom in the sense of the ethic proposed here is a characteristic of structured social relationships, and does not isolate the individual from the influence of social constraints. It is not urged that individuals be free from constraints, but rather that societies have social structures that optimize alternatives open to all societal members.

Second, the term *freedom* is not meant to denote a *freedom to restrict* the alternatives open to all by an individual or group. The term *freedom* is often used rhetorically in this sense, as in "we are free to do as we please, and my freedom to establish a monopoly or discriminate against certain groups should not be abridged." The orientation proposed here urges the optimization of alternatives open to *every* individual, and thus seeks a *general* optimization of freedom.

This suggests that any action designed to bring about a general optimization of alternatives may actually decrease alternatives for some particular individuals or groups. Thus, for example, economic freedom might at first be seen to permit the alternative of monopolistic practices. On the contrary, monopolies would not be implied, because they eliminate both the alternatives of those who wish to enter the market and the alternatives of those consumers who wish to purchase within the market. (While it seems reasonable that monopolistic practices would bring about a general decrease rather than a general increase in alternatives, whether they actually do or not can be treated as an empirical question.) Thus, it may be necessary to eliminate one alternative in order to optimize alternatives generally. In short, the orientation suggests that every individual's freedom should be optimized as much as possible without his jeopardizing the freedom of others.

Ultimately, then, what is proposed is: *the optimization of alternatives open to every individual compatible with equal optimization of alternatives open to all*—each individual's freedom should be continually increased up to the point that it begins to interfere with the *optimization of freedom of others*. (Even when not stated explicitly on the following pages, the rider may be assumed to be implicitly present.) This orientation clearly suggests optimizing freedom not only for elites, or a powerless minority, or even a popular majority, but for all individuals.

Implications of the Skeptic's View

Anticipating the next chapter, we should discuss the implications of the skeptic's view for a goal orientation of societal survival.

Some sociologists might argue that sociology should orient its decision making according to societal survival. That is, all decisions involved in the search for and employment of sociological knowledge should be aimed at developing and promoting the likelihood of societal survival. An adherent of the skeptic's view would probably counter that while most take the goal of survival for granted, its value is still not demonstrable and thus assumptive. So, it also depends on persuasive reasons for its adoption despite its "obvious" value. One compelling reason for a survival orientation is that it is clearly necessary for a society to optimize its alternatives. The survival of society might not be argued to be of value in itself, but only insofar as it allowed the possibility of freedom.

The promotion of social structures that optimize alternatives is argued to be a unique goal, worthy of consideration by the sociological profession, because it minimally imposes a conception of good on others by widening areas of choice in which societal members may actualize their own conceptions of what is good.

Five

The Naturalistic–
Evolutionary View

Contradicting the skeptic's view are numerous "naturalistic" positions which generally argue that knowledge claims can serve as a basis for making value claims. While they disagree about which types of facts should act as the basic referents (for example, pleasure, desire, or need), they would undoubtedly concur in rejecting any view which denied facts a central role in the justification of a goal orientation (for discussions of major naturalistic positions, see Hancock, 1974, pp. 18–40, 58–86; Adams, 1960; Perry, 1954; Frankena, 1973, pp. 96–102). In some form, all of these positions identify statements of what is good or obligatory or what ought to be with some natural object or property. The term *natural* here refers to "something of which the existence is admittedly an object of experience" (Moore, 1903, p. 38). As such, it refers to objects and properties which are capable of being verified as facts. "If we consider whether any object is of such a nature that it may be said to exist now, to have existed, or to be about to exist, then we may know that that object is a natural object, and that nothing of which this is not true, is a natural object" (Moore, 1903, p. 40). Further, the reference in these views to natural objects and properties is in terms of basic or highest-level values rather than low-level values:

> One way of putting [the] question is to ask whether our basic ethical judgments can be justified in any objective way similar to those in which our factual judgments can be justified. It is, therefore, by a natural impulse that many philosophers have sought to show that certain ethical judgments are actually rooted in fact or, as it used to be put, "the nature of things." . . . Opponents have . . . countered that this cannot be done, since one cannot get an Ought out of an Is or a Value out of a Fact. Now, we do sometimes seem to justify an ethical judgment by an appeal to fact. Thus, we say that a certain act is wrong because it injures someone. . . . However, it becomes clear on a moment's thought that our conclusion does not rest on our factual premise alone. . . . We are tacitly assuming that injurious acts are wrong, which is a moral principle. . . . In such cases, then, we are not justifying our ethical judgment by reference to fact alone but also by reference to a *more basic* ethical premise. The question is whether our *most basic* ethical or value premises can be derived logically from factual ones alone [Frankena, 1973, pp. 96–97].

While many of the naturalistic formulations are worthy of consideration, only one has been singled out for examination here. This is the evolutionary approach that has been forcefully argued by Waddington in his book *The Ethical Animal* (1960). This formulation most successfully circumvents major arguments that have been lodged against most other naturalistic formulations.

Most of these formulations can be said to take one of two general approaches. The first attempts to derive logically conclusions that contain terms such as *good* or *ought* from other premises that do not contain them. These approaches are accused of being fallacious in that they make a leap in logic that is not acceptable according to usual practices. That is, they try to argue, "A equals B, therefore A equals C," without including premises that logically connect A to C. The second general naturalistic approach, rather than attempting to logically derive an ought from an is, attempts to define the good in terms of some natural property, such as the "pleasurable." This approach is argued either (1) to be circular, in that what we wish to ascertain is defined into existence and often later treated as having been demonstrated, or (2) to be begging the question in that, for example, once *good* is defined as "pleasurable" we may still ask if any particular pleasurable act is also good. This latter question can only be answered by referring to the term which we were initially trying to define. Waddington's evolutionary formulation takes neither of these approaches and thus avoids these serious criticisms.

Waddington's Naturalistic-Evolutionary View

The perspectives suggested in Waddington's *The Ethical Animal* (1967) offer numerous challenges to the skeptic's view of the basis for choosing a nonepistemic decision orientation.* Had Waddington read Chapter Four of this work, he would have probably criticized the skeptic's view for implying that man's intellect stands apart from nature which misrepresents the surrounding circumstances of life. "The human intellect is an instrument which has been produced during the course of evolution, primarily by the agency of natural selection, supplemented by the specifically human evolutionary processes which we shall discuss later. Like all products of evolution, it has been moulded by the necessity to fit in with—or rather, to put it more actively, to cope with—the rest of the natural world. Its function is not to produce a God-like vision of the human situation seen from the stand-point above and outside the turmoil of actual life" (Waddington, 1967, p. 19). By preventing our

* While this brief review shall attempt to convey the flavor of Waddington's arguments, the reader is referred to the original to gain fuller appreciation of the richness of this scholar's insights.

knowledge of the world from serving as the basis for a goal orientation, the skeptic's view illegitimately sets man apart from nature. It
might be further argued that adherents to the skeptic's view see "a
radical distinction between man and the rest of the world" (p. 76),
viewing man as acting independently on something essentially foreign to himself.

Waddington would further disagree that the choice of an
orientation which embodies basic values and ethical considerations
can only have an assumptive grounding. Basic facts for Waddington are the attempts of a species to survive and its evolution. Further, human ethical systems are products of and play an important
role in human survival and evolution. So, rather than asserting that
there is only an assumptive basis for the choice of ethical systems,
Waddington argues "that the framework within which one can
carry on a rational discussion of different systems of ethics, and
make comparisons of their various merits and demerits is to be
found in consideration of animal and human evolution" (p. 23).

Waddington states that the situation for societies is similar
to that of the newborn human infant, who develops into an "ethicis-
ing being" (one who is highly conscious of ethics) not wholly because of intrinsic forces, but as a result of interaction with external
circumstances. Ethical feelings and beliefs are adopted because they
are functional in assuring a child's survival and promoting his
relationships with others (pp. 25–27). Societal ethical systems have
also evolved in the process of interaction with social and physical
environments and have survived because they have promoted societal survival and evolutionary developments. If we grant that the
function of ethical beliefs is to promote survival and evolutionary
development, we have a criterion for choosing between ethical
systems.

> Now, once we have assigned the functions to a
> general type of activity we have a rational criterion
> against which to judge any particular example of that
> activity. To say that something has a function is not
> merely to assign causal efficacy to it, but implies fur-
> ther that the causal network of which it is a part has
> as a whole some general character. A particular ex-

ample of the activity can then be judged by how well
it brings about the realization of that character.

It is a criterion of this kind which we can hope
to apply to human ethical beliefs. We have first to try to
ascertain the general character of human evolution or,
indeed of animal evolution as a whole. We have then
to inquire of any particular ethical belief which comes
to our attention, how effective it is in mediating this
empirically ascertained course of evolutionary change
[pp. 29–30].

Thus for Waddington, the choice and justification of any
particular belief is how well it fulfills its functions of promoting
survival and evolution.

Waddington's Avoidance of the Usual Criticisms

As was pointed out at the beginning of this chapter, many
naturalistic formulations have attempted to logically derive ethical
statements from statements of fact, which have been accused of
making what Moore calls the "naturalistic fallacy." These attacks
find their roots in the writings of Hume (especially *A Treatise of
Human Nature,* Book 3, Part I):

> In every system of morality which I have
> hitherto met with, I have always remarked that the
> author proceeds for some time in ordinary ways of rea-
> soning, and establishes the being of a god or makes
> observations concerning human affairs; when of a sud-
> den I am surprised to find that instead of the usual
> copulations of propositions is and is not, I meet with no
> proposition that is not concerned with an ought or an
> ought not. This change is imperceptible; but is how-
> ever of the last consequence. For as this ought or ought
> not expresses some new relation of affirmation, it is
> necessary that it should be observed and explained; and
> at the same time that a reason should be given for what
> seems altogether inconceivable; how this new relation
> can be a deduction from others that are entirely differ-
> ent from it [in Waddington, pp. 50–51].

This criticism—that one cannot legitimately deduce an ought from an is—can probably be applied to many formulations. However, it does not seem applicable to Waddington's formulation, because he is not maintaining that the good is deducible from facts but rather that ethical systems can be chosen and justified by referring to a factual criterion, namely, their functionality in promoting survival and evolution. While it is widely assumed that some high-level value must be the final arbiter in such choices, Waddington argues that a "supra-ethical" criterion can just as readily be a set of fact. "However, for my major purpose the validity or otherwise of the refutation of the naturalistic fallacy is irrelevant. I wish to maintain that it is possible to discuss, and perhaps to discover, a criterion which is not of an ethical nature, but is, if you wish, of a supra-ethical character; a criterion, that is to say, which would make it possible to decide whether a certain ethical system of values is in some definite and important sense preferable to another" (pp. 54–55).

Using a naturalistic-evolutionary criterion does not confer on the chosen ethical system any ultimate value. Put another way, the only good that the resultant ethical system possesses is a "good of a kind." When we say, "This is a good gun," we imply neither that guns are good nor that the given gun has an ultimate value. Rather, we are saying that the gun performs its functions well, such as shooting straight and having high velocity. Similarly, we might say that the use of an evolutionary criterion does not add any ultimate value to the chosen ethical system, but that the resultant system performs well the function of ethical systems generally in that it effectively promotes survival and evolution.

In a similar fashion, Waddington also avoids the criticisms of formulations that define the good in natural terms. The definist formulations are often accused of being circular in that they begin by defining the good in natural terms, and then later assert that these natural properties or objects are good and are to be valued. Waddington does not define *good* or *right* as "more evolved," and points out that there is really no resemblance between the characteristic we have in mind when we use the terms *good* or *right* and that which we have in mind when we use the term *more evolved*. "If we ask ourselves what 'more evolved' means, we should find in it, I think, two main elements: (1) that conduct so described comes, in time, after a process of evolution of more or less duration, and (2) that it has as a characteristic which usually emerges in the course of evolution, that of being complex, in comparison with the simple activities which appear in an early stage of evolution. And it is surely clear that neither temporal posteriority nor complexity, nor the union of the two, is that which we mean to refer to when we use the term *right* or *obligatory*" (p. 51). If the factual terms and value terms are not interdefined, there are no grounds for accusing this naturalistic-evolutionary formulation of circularity.

What Waddington is presenting, then, is a form of argument that is radically different from classical naturalistic presentations. In fact, we should perhaps take note of the difference by using terms such as *quasi-naturalist* or *second-order naturalist* when referring to a position such as Waddington's. (The term *quasi-naturalist* was presumably coined by Brandt [1959, pp. 265–267] in discussing his own "qualified attitude method" of ethical justification.) At the same time, we may reserve the term *naturalist* or the phrase *first-order naturalist* when referring to classical naturalists. First-order naturalists normally define certain ethical terms by referring to natural terms. They do this explicitly in definist views, or implicitly when deducing ethical statements from factual ones (where the implicit definition is actually what allows the deduction). In either case, once the naturalistic definition is agreed on, some ultimate, substantive ethical principle follows immediately from it. The proposed ethical principle, then, is circular, or true by definition. As Brandt points out, "Some naturalist definitions, like the proposal that 'x is worthwhile in itself' means 'x is pleasant,' have the consequence that substantive ethical principles are true by definition (in this case 'something is worthwhile in itself if and only if it is pleasant')" (1959, p. 266). A second-order or quasi-naturalistic position, on the other hand, does not define ethical terms by referring to naturalistic ones, but rather defines naturalistically a method for choosing between ethical systems. Further, no important substantive ethical principles follow immediately from that method by definition. A first-order naturalist might have said, "By *good* we mean 'x is that which leads to survival,' " and have concluded "x is good if it leads to survival." In contrast, second-order naturalists such as Waddington define a method for choosing between statements naturalistically. In particular, Waddington argues that our criterion for choosing between ethical systems is the extent to which they fulfill their function of promoting survival and furthering evolution, which does not automatically entail some particular substantive ethical principle. In fact, since a substantive good is not being defined, the criticisms aimed at first-order naturalists may best be considered irrelevant, rather than incorrect, when applied to Waddington.

> To a theory which attempted to discover a criterion for judging between ethical systems the refutation of the naturalistic fallacy would be largely beside the point. We should be denying Moore's contention that "the question, how 'good' is to be defined, is the most fundamental question in all Ethics." Instead our standpoint would be somewhat nearer to that ascribed to Kant by Broad, when he wrote: "Kant would say, I think, that it is no more the business of ethics to provide rules of conduct than is the business of logic to provide arguments. The business of ethics is to provide a test for rules of conduct, just as it is the business of logic to provide a test for argument." But we should be carrying the argument one step further. Where Kant was seeking to establish some particular ethical belief as a criterion by which to judge between alternative rules of conduct, we should be attempting to establish some general principle of wisdom as a criterion for judging between alternative ethical beliefs [Waddington, pp. 53–54].

Given that Waddington has avoided the fundamental criticisms of most naturalistic positions, what set of facts can be considered as the criterion?

Naturalistic-Evolutionary Basis for a Choice Between Ethical Systems

Those maintaining a naturalistic-evolutionary view would not feel a need to justify the value of continued survival, while the skeptic would argue that justification was necessary. Rather, while naturalistic-evolutionary adherents might acknowledge that some species and societies have not maintained attempts to continue existence, they would add that the basic fact of biological knowledge is that every known species and probably every human being has been guided by the continuation of existence. A second,

> unavoidable biological fact is that of evolution. For at least the last hundred years, since Darwin wrote, biologists have had to consider all living things, including man, as being produced in such a way as to bring its results into adjustment with the circumstances surrounding it. It is by now absolutely conventional and a matter of first principles to consider the whole physiological and sensory apparatus of any living thing as a result of a process which tailors it into conformity with the situation with which the organism will have to deal. The same principle undoubtedly applies to behavioral characteristics, and there is no obvious reason to deny it out of hand in relation to intellectual and even moral characteristics in those organisms which exhibit them [Waddington, pp. 72–73].

From a naturalistic-evolutionary perspective, then, survival and evolution are the primary facts that should serve as criterion in choosing and justifying a value system. In accordance with this view, an orientation should be chosen and is most justified which maximally promotes survival and evolution. In reality, evolution is not seen as a distinct criterion apart from survival, but rather the two are seen as highly interdependent. Evolution in a most general sense is molded by and a product of survival, and evolutionary developments may be said to generally increase the probability of survival.

Waddington also offers a more specific analysis of the biological evolutionary system with special emphasis on the genetic system (pp. 85–100), which, although it provides an excellent discussion of knowledge and recent insights, need not concern us here. However, one recent insight, which is generally credited to Darlington, will be of particular interest to social scientists. While biologists generally acknowledge that species are evolving, only recently have they recognized that the genetic systems responsible for evolutionary development are themselves evolving. The genetic system is that whole complex of processes which creates and transmits hereditary variation. Waddington maintains that "there will be a natural selection in favor of more efficient systems which most effectively throw up hereditary variations of the kind natural selection will favor" (p. 101). While a large number of different genetic systems have been recognized in subhuman species, the most radically different appears to be the "socio-genetic" system of human evolution.

While the teaching of younger members of the population by older members plays a relatively minor role in subhuman species, it plays a major role in the human species, and many modes of information transmission and reception have developed. "What we have here amounts to a new mode of hereditary transmission. It is true that this cannot transmit a new variation in our bodily structure as do the genes, but it can transmit conceptual knowledge, beliefs, feelings, aesthetic creations and other mental phenomena together with a vast variety of non-human artefacts" (p. 102). Dobzhansky (1956) and others have come to agree with Darlington, Julian Huxley, and Waddington that man's development of a cultural system constitutes a mode of evolution which was previously nonexistent and which is a significant step in the evolution of evolutionary mechanisms.

This socio-genetic system is quite similar to the genetic system in some respects. At an abstract level genes can be said to be primarily transmitters of genetic information from one generation to the next. The socio-genetic mechanism also passes information to succeeding generations. "Another writer trained in the classical doctrines of genetics, Kenneth Mather, has recently expressed the same ideas as follows: 'Ideas have many of the properties we find in genes. . . . They are transmissible, and therefore permanent in the same sense as genes, they vary and they are selected. Because they vary and are selected, the caucus of ideas and concepts on which the structure of society depends is not only capable of evolution but must evolve. . . . This social evolution . . . has come to overlay and obscure the genetical variation which we see when we look within societies' " (Waddington, p. 106).

The socio-genetic system has perhaps come to "overlay and

obscure" the genetic due to important differences between the two. Socio-genetic transmission is not limited only to biological relatives; information can be transmitted and received by a wide variety of societal members. Further, the information is not received "entirely or even mainly at one point in the life history of new generations." As a result, "we have, as it were, an enormous expansion and multiplication of paragenetic transmission" (p. 113). The result is an overshadowing of the genetic system, and as a result knowledge, technology, and social structures have evolved at a tremendous pace in recent history, with relatively slight changes in body structure. This does not mean that the genetic system is no longer operating in man—it is; the evolutionary capabilities of each evolutionary system over time differ. What is presented, then, is a new evolutionary system that is not merely analogous to the genetic system, but a new system of evolution that is both a product of the genetic system and continues to operate with it.

Before we analyze the implications of the naturalistic-evolutionary perspective on the choice of an orientation, we will digress in order to suggest some of the criticisms that an adherent of the skeptic's view might advance against this position as a basis for such a choice.

Criticisms of the Naturalistic-Evolutionary Position

Since major criticisms have been already advanced against the skeptic's view, it seems appropriate to consider potential criticisms of the naturalistic-evolutionary position. These criticisms are suggested only briefly, since we are not attempting to choose between these bases for the choice of an orientation. Even in light of the criticisms advanced, each position will be likely to attract a significant number of professionals to warrant their consideration as a possible basis for an orientation for sociology.

The first criticism that a skeptic might offer is that in choosing an orientation for guiding important areas of human behavior, it is inappropriate to have as a criterion a fact or set of facts that is uncoupled with some statement of high-level values. Even if the skeptic admitted that the criterion was truly factual and avoided the problems of fallacious or circular reasoning, he might argue that high-level values still ought to be the final referent. Here the skeptic may doggedly ask, even of such a basic fact as existence, "Should we value it?" Even Dobzhansky, an acknowledged supporter of evolutionary ethics and considered by Waddington as "perhaps the most distinguished evolutionist of today" (p. 105), points out that even if we were provided with complete knowledge of the direction of human evolution, "Just why should we take for granted that this direction, which we have not chosen, is good? The very fact that man knows that he has evolved and is evolving means that he is able to contemplate speeding up his evolution, slowing it down, stopping it altogether, or changing its direction. And his increasing knowledge and understanding of evolution may enable him to translate his thoughts into reality. Despite any exhortations to the contrary, man will not permanently deny himself the right to question the wisdom of anything, including the wisdom of his evolutionary direction" (Dobzhansky, 1956, p. 129).

Thus the skeptic, insisting on the inclusion of questions of ultimate value, draws the argument back into the web of infinite regression and assumptive validity. In fairness to Waddington and others sympathetic to his position, the idea that basic values, rather than basic facts, should be the court of last appeal is debatable at best. While it may be asserted "that an ethical value is *ex officio* the overriding principle of policy, and can be judged only in terms of something which has still a higher value" (Waddington, p. 55), this need not be automatically assumed. However, the idea that certain basic facts or wisdom should act as a supraethical criterion over basic values also need not be automatically assumed. Both positions are probably best viewed as high-level assertions or assumptions.

A second objection the skeptic may raise is whether survival of a species is truly problematic, or whether the more realistic threats are to valued ways of existence. Humanity's adaptability makes serious threats to its survival improbable. As Waddington points out, "the recent metamorphosis in the human condition has been extraordinarily rapid. Four lifetimes could not cover the essential transition. Man's adaptability is so great that we often fail to realize the magnitude of this change" (p. 13). Even if there were an all-out nuclear war tomorrow, undoubtedly the species would continue to exist in some form. The skeptic would argue that the question lies in the value of the form of survival.

This objection may be stated in more positive terms: Many of us wish to do more than survive—we wish to somehow "improve" our condition. At several points Waddington explains his position by referring to an analogy of physical health (for example, see pp. 29–31 or p. 59). Thus for the nutritionist to criticize eating habits, he determines the function of eating and what diets satisfy this function; then he examines the particular diet. What we have, in Waddington's terms, is a normative criterion. We find out what is statistically normal and use this as a grounds for criticizing abnormality.

The criterion we are applying here is one of general accordance with the nature of the world as we observe it. If any individual approaches a nutritionist and says that he prefers to grow in an abnormal and unhealthy manner, the nutritionist can do no more than tell him that if he does so he will be out of step with nature (Waddington, p. 30). The problem is that many people may wish to be abnormal in a positive sense, such as an athlete. A view tied to statistical normality allows no possibility of being extraordinary or exceptional. Similarly, we may wish our society to change in positively valued ways apart from a greater likelihood of continued existence. While it may be argued that the idea of evolution implies improvement or change in positively valued ways as well as survival, if we shift the definition of evolution and embed more value terms within it, then we are guilty of the naturalistic fallacy discussed earlier in this chapter. In particular, we would incorporate the circularity of the definist position.

The skeptic might also argue that we lack sufficient knowledge or wisdom for choosing and justifying an ethical system. Our knowledge of the evolutionary process in general, and human evolution in particular, has passed through numerous radical changes. Yet each stage of knowledge that was later discredited was once as strongly accepted as facts as are our current notions. Consider earlier instances of evolutionary ethics. Waddington points out that "Herbert Spencer and others advanced theories of a 'Social Darwinist' kind, involving such notions as the inevitability of progress and the application of such slogans as the survival of the fittest or the struggle for existence to human social affairs. These theories have been so completely discredited that at this time little further needs to be said about them" (p. 23).

Such "notions" were not simply put forth as the conjecture of a few, but rather were widely held as facts. The question is whether our knowledge and conceptual frameworks accurately reflect actual processes, so that what remains is to fill in the gaps, as opposed to revamping our major concepts. If the answer is no, do we wish to have our lives directed by such knowledge?

In one sense this is an unfair criticism. While numerous applications of the criterion would be affected, some kind of evolution seems unmistakable, and thus the criterion would ultimately remain unchanged. The criticism is also unfair if applied to the lack of knowledge for applying the criterion, for the application of any ethical system, even when chosen according to high-level values, depends on knowledge of what is, was, and will be the case and thus falls prey to the same criticism.

Finally, the skeptic might state that although the general nature of evolutionary change is progressive, any particular stage need not be (Waddington, pp. 125–126). The decision seems to be made in large part as to whether the change at any given stage is in line with the species' "character." For example, the evolution of the horse from small four-toed animals to animals with long legs and single toes involved a series of improvements that enhanced their general character or organization. In particular, their basic character relies for survival "on their fleetness of foot to escape their enemies" (Waddington, pp. 126–127). This conception of the species' character makes sense, but the problem is that it is arrived at retrospectively. If evolution had proceeded differently, say, with horses' toes becoming claws or their hide becoming increasingly tough and impenetrable, we would also consider these changes as improvements, but with a very different understanding of the species' character.

Moreover, if we truly accept the idea of evolution, there is no reason to assume that there exists some initial species character that is continually refined. It seems equally reasonable to consider the possibility that each species' basic character or organization is *also* evolving. That is, each species is not so much becoming more of what it is, but is becoming more of what it is becoming. If, in fact, a species' character is also evolving and we cannot know it at some evolutionary endpoint (should there be one), there is a serious difficulty in choosing a point of reference.

Other criticisms could be lodged against the naturalistic-evolutionary view, just as they could against the skeptic's view. It is highly unlikely that any position could be developed in this area that would be beyond criticism. Both positions have sufficient merit that one could reasonably hold either. Again, we do not attempt to choose between them here, but rather to consider their implications for the choice of an orientation, since each will likely attract a large number of adherents among sociologists. Also, a choice is not made between them for perhaps a more important reason. In the discussion of the first criticism concerning the choice between a highest-level value and a supraethical fact as the final criterion for justifying an orientation, it was suggested that the disagreement was at such a basic level that it may be unresolvable and may be best considered an assertion. When the two positions are taken as wholes the same type of problem arises: They may be so basic that it may be impossible to get outside them to choose between them. The term *view* was chosen in describing them because they may be conceived of as world views. More particularly, the two positions seem to hinge on different perceptions of being. Waddington (p. 54) seems to suggest that "The validity of Hume's argument that one cannot logically proceed from an 'Is' to an 'Ought' depends entirely on what is the content of the notion conveyed by 'Is.' If one conceives of existence as, to put it crudely, Newtonism space-time with some billiard balls flying round in it, then clearly neither 'oughts' nor 'owes' can be logically deduced. But if, to take another extreme, existence is considered as the manifestation of the nature of a beneficent Deity, quite other consequences would follow."

If the two positions are in fact two very different world views embodying different perceptions of ontology or metaphysics, this writer is ill equipped to suggest the mechanism by which we can choose between them. Further, while someone will undoubtedly attempt to do so, it is unclear how one can proclaim "they are both right," although both positions similarly avoid arguing in terms of ultimate values. At any rate, it seems worthwhile to ex-

amine the implications of the naturalistic-evolutionary perspective
on choosing a goal orientation as we did in Chapter Five for the
skeptic's view.

Implications of the Naturalistic-Evolutionary View

From the preceding pages it has become clear that according
to the naturalistic-evolutionary formulation, the primary criterion
for choosing an orientation is how well it fulfills its function of contributing to the survival and evolution of societies or the species.
(The exact referent of the criterion is not totally clear. It is variously
suggested to be societies, the human species as a whole, and the
evolution of all species as a whole.) In the previous chapter it was
suggested that if the skeptic's view was accepted, it would support
the choice of an orientation of optimizing alternatives open to all
individuals, because such an orientation mitigates the effects of
unwarranted value imposition. It is suggested here that even if the
radically different naturalistic-evolutionary perspective was adopted,
it would still support an optimizing orientation. Just as was the case
for the skeptic's view, the naturalistic-evolutionary perspective is not
said to logically entail the proposed orientation—it is probably impossible to show logical entailment of any such high-level goal
orientation. Rather, the naturalistic-evolutionary view seems to
strongly suggest and support the proposed orientation. At minimum,
the optimizing orientation seems congruent with the naturalistic-evolutionary perspective. In particular, the optimization of alternatives
is congruent with the dominant features of human, and to some
extent nonhuman, evolution as we understand it, and it is likely to
increase the probability of the continuing evolution and survival of
societies and species. Before discussing this, two possible lines of
reasoning, which will not be pursued, should be briefly mentioned.

The first such line of reasoning is that if there is some dominant, discernible feature of the character of the human species, it is
a desire and a love for freedom (doubtlessly there are a multitude
of other possibilities). It might be argued in line with Kelman's
(1965, p. 35) suggestion "that the desire to choose represents a
universal human need, which manifests itself under different historical circumstances (not only under conditions of oppression)."

The second line of reasoning is that if the evolutionary course that mankind follows is unalterable (except, perhaps, changing its speed), then on the whole human evolution is moving toward freedom as an endpoint, and we should accept this or speed it up.

Both of these positions, while defensible, require a vast amount of research; even then they would probably be exceedingly difficult to demonstrate conclusively. The lines of reasoning and evidence that follow are also not conclusive, but the evidence from some of the most noted evolutionary scholars of today—Waddington, Dobzhansky, and others—strongly suggests and supports the optimization orientation proposed here.

Waddington starts his chapter on "The Course of Evolutionary Progress" by pointing out that while the evolutionary system as a whole is characterized by an inherent tendency toward progressive improvement through natural selection, "this does not imply that such progressive improvements always occur in every evolutionary sequence" (p. 125). (Waddington's use of the term *progress* is unfortunate because its common usage has made it somewhat vague and it often carries ideological overtones. However, we use it to remain consistent with Waddington.) At present, the products of evolution are usually considered by biologists in terms of three basic categories.

> The three categories are: (1) *Stasigenesis,* the attainment of a biologically satisfactory condition which persists unchanged through long evolutionary periods. Striking examples are provided by such well-known cases as the Brachiopod Lingula which seems to have remained unaltered since the Ordovician [Period.] . . . (2) *Cladogenesis,* the evolution of a diversified range of species and genera all falling within a single organizational type. . . . The appearance of a multiplicity of, for instance, Dipteran flies, or deer, or land snails, are just a few random examples. (3) *Anagenesis,* the appearance of something which can be recognized as an improvement over the previously existing type. It is the concept of anagenesis which requires the greatest attention in the present context [i.e., explaining evolutionary progress; Waddington, p. 126].

Waddington explains anagenesis using the horse as an example '(pp. 126–127). The evolution of the horse proceeded through various stages, or, in Julian Huxley's term, "grades" (levels through which successive improvements have passed). The evolutionary sequence began with small four-toed animals that grazed on grasses and bushes and survived by relying on speed to escape from their enemies. For the horse, evolutionary improvements included the lengthening of legs, gradually shifting from four toes to one, which increased running efficiency, and developing longer and stronger teeth for chewing grass. "Changes of this kind are clearly improvements in efficiency by the frame of reference given by the three general types of organization. They constitute anagenesis" (Waddington, p. 127).

However, while this evolutionary development was an improvement from a narrow point of reference, it closed off a large number of patterns of evolutionary development that were previously possible.

> Now, what is an improvement for a horse may very well be something quite different from another point of view. The horse anagenesis has in fact led to a highly specialized creature with only one toe on each foot, highly fitted for carrying out one type of life but quite unable to earn its living in nature except in that specialized manner. If one considers from a long run point of view the evolution of land-living mammals in general, it becomes apparent that the course which evolution has followed in the horse group has cut it off from the possibility of following some of the lines of change that were potentially open to its remote ancestors, for instance the development of the manipulative hand. Anagenesis may therefore lead to an evolutionary dead end [Waddington, p. 127].

While Huxley used the term *anagenesis* in a very broad way to refer to any improvement over the previous type, Rensch, who originally coined the term, used it more specifically to mean "an improvement in grade which did not, at least to any marked degree, restrict the potentialities for future evolutionary developments"

(Waddington, p. 128). Waddington suggests that we may continue to use Huxley's broader usage if we "distinguish two types of anagenetic change: a 'closing' type which leads to improvement with one type of biological organization but a restriction of future potentialities, and an 'opening' type which involves improvement but no noticeable restriction" (p. 128).

Waddington offers several examples of opening anagenesis. For instance, the development of a special part of the external or internal body surface to fulfill the function of respiratory exchange, such as gills or lungs, posed no obvious limitations and permitted new possible uses of the rest of the body surface, such as protection or absorption of food materials. The primary criterion in assessing whether an evolutionary development is of the opening type is whether it increases the possibilities of evolutionary alteration. An additional example of opening anagenesis has occurred in the evolution of genetic systems themselves. Diploid sexual reproduction can be seen as anagenesis of the opening type compared with systems of self-reproduction and mutation. However, since the development of diploid sexual reproduction, with one exception, all the more recent developments in genetic systems (such as unisexual or parthogenetic and hermaphrodite reproduction) have been of the closing type, leading to restrictive specializations rather than opening new possibilities of advance. The exception is the evolution of the characteristically human socio-genetic system (Waddington, pp. 129–131). The concept of opening anagenesis is crucial in understanding both human evolution and the modern view of evolution in general.

> It is clear that for a discussion of biological evolution in relation to man and human evolution, it is the occurrence of anagenesis which takes the center stage. Stasigenesis is in some ways a failure of evolution. . . . If nothing but stasigenesis had happened in the organic world, the concept of evolution would never have been invented. Cladogenesis—the appearance of diversity—is, of course, a real evolutionary phenomenon. The notion could indeed be taken to cover the whole of evolution, if we were convinced that no anagenesis had occurred. If there are any biologists

who, while accepting the notion of evolution, reject
that of evolutionary progress, they must presumably
consider that all the results of evolution can be placed
under this heading. Such a position would, however,
be a very extreme and peculiar one, so far removed
from a single interpretation of the evidence that one
could scarcely avoid the suspicion that anyone advancing it was doing so merely in order to provide grounds
for some future argument. I think that all biologists
who have no ulterior ends in view have always, from
the time of Aristotle, agreed that one can discuss a real
hierarchy or progression in the forms of the organic
world [Waddington, pp. 133–134].

Further, there is general agreement on how the hierarchy is
arranged, at least in terms of broad categories. While introductory
texts offer detailed outlines, it is generally agreed that at the bottom
are bacteria and viruses, then protozoa, then sponges, then mollusks,
on up through insects and finally the vertebrates at the top. Within
that group is a clear progression from various types of fish, through
the amphibians, to the reptiles, birds, and mammals. This hierarchy
may be explained in terms of the different points of development at
which opening anagenesis ceased and closing anagenesis became
dominant:

The existence of a clear-cut hierarchical order
which we interpret as evolutionary anagenesis, within
single groups such as arthropods, forces us to remind
ourselves of the distinction between opening and closing
anagenesis. Evolution from a primitive anthropod to
a highly evolved insect such as a fly or a bee has undoubtedly involved the real improvement of the arthro-
pod type of organization, but this improvement has at
the same time brought with it limitations which render
indefinite further improvements impossible.

Similar considerations probably apply to all the
major groups of the animal kingdom. In each of them
evolution has produced, by anagenesis, the improvement of one particular type of biological organization,
but in doing so has gradually eliminated various other

possibilities. Within each group anagenesis has been in the main closing anagenesis [Waddington, pp. 134–135].

Continuing evolution, then, demands an opening anagenesis in which structures remain open to, rather than restricted from, possible avenues of future development and thus structures that do not perfect some particular form of organization. Any orientation that is to be chosen and justified on the basis of a naturalistic-evolutionary view must be congruent with this basic evolutionary fact and must function to promote evolution by promoting opening anagenesis. As Waddington states, "The major point about opening anagenesis, which is important to the thesis I am advancing here that there has been evolutionary progress, is that it has occurred. This I take to be established by the consensus of general biological opinion" (p. 136).

The proposed orientation requires optimizing alternatives, which implies optimizing possibilities of choice and therefore courses of development. The orientation was introduced by comparing it with its opposite, the minimization of alternatives. The latter orientation seeks societies that minimize alternatives in order to establish a particular conception of the good at the expense of alternative conceptions. Such a society would attempt "the perfection of one particular type of organization." This could constitute closing anagenesis because it does not leave open the possibility of future advance. Again the primary choice seems to be between societies that are organized to keep open and expand avenues of development, change, and potential advance and those that strive to organize and develop in order to actualize some particular value and thus eliminate other potential lines of development.

Further, we know that the dominant mode of human evolutionary progress is socio-genetic. In this mode anagenetic, or improving, developments are carried out by the creation, transmission, and reception of ideas and emotions as well as nonintellectual artifacts. Widening the areas of choice open to societal members increases the avenues of divergent experience and exploration. These in turn increase the probability of the creative production of new ideas, emotions, and artifacts, which can then be infused into the evolutionary development of society as a whole. The central feature to be recognized about the optimizing orientation is that it optimizes potentiality.

The proposed orientation cannot be proven conclusively to be the sole orientation that meets the criterion of promoting evolutionary advance. However, if the central feature of continued evolutionary advance is opening anagenesis (suggested by biological opinion), and if this orientation will better fulfill the function of ethical systems promoting evolutionary advance by promoting opening anagenesis, the profession can justifiably choose the optimizing orientation as its goal orientation. While further investigation must be devoted to the topic, our current understanding of opening anagenesis seems at this time both highly suggestive and supportive of the proposed orientation or some form of it that optimizes alternatives.

We may further consider whether the proposed orientation best increases the probability of societal (and thus species') survival. Obviously, the factors involved are very complex and our knowledge far from complete. Still, we may hypothesize that, in general, the societies that have the highest probability of survival are those societies that have optimized alternatives open to their members.

The modern understanding of the survival of species does not see natural selection as favoring species that possess innately superior characteristics; rather it favors species that adapt to or, more actively, best cope with their external circumstances.

In opposition to the optimizing orientation an argument might be presented along the following lines: (1) A given society has certain external circumstances, such as its social and physical environments and its available resources, (2) social structures of a society oriented to a specified value best fit in or cope with these external circumstances; (3) therefore, we should accept an orientation which promotes societal organization in line with this value; for (4) perfection of this organization increases the probability of survival.

If these premises are accepted, the choice of such a value orientation would be reasonable if it is assumed that external circumstances are primarily static. However, the contrary view is that environments are not static, but are highly dynamic and changing in important ways. If this is the case, societies that adapt to specific external conditions and allow one value to dominate, may become maladapted if the environment changes considerably. The problems of specialized organization have been clearly seen in experiments on other forms of life, as Dobzhansky points out. While it is true that adaptation to the environment by means of genotypic specialization is advantageous in a relatively constant environment, "the drawback of genotypic specialization and fixation is that the possibilities of adaptation to environmental changes become severely limited. Numerous and ingenious experiments have shown that when an animal is placed in novel environments, its innate behavior loses its 'wisdom.' The animal is likely to do exactly the wrong thing, damaging its own chance of survival or that of its offspring" (Dobzhansky, 1956, p. 95).

Although restricting alternatives to societal members may be more adaptive in a particular unchanging environment, these same restrictions may threaten societal survival within a changing social and physical environment. In contrast, the optimization of alternatives increases the probability that the society as a whole will have open to it behaviors and structures that remain adaptive to and can cope with the changing environment. While it may seem extreme to discuss the possibility of an end to societal or human existence, "the geological strata of the earth's crust contain fossilized remains of countless thousands of species that became extinct without issue. . . . They became extinct mostly because natural selection made them too specialized to live in environments which were only temporary" (Dobzhansky, 1956, p. 84).

This chapter presents a view upon which to base a choice of an orientation that is radically different from and critical of the skeptic's view. Even though they represent highly divergent world views, the optimization of alternatives orientation that was originally presented as congruent with the skeptic's view is not only not rejected by the naturalistic-evolutionary view, it can be argued to be suggested and supported by it. This is not to say that some other orientation could not be supported by either position, but rather that the proposed orientation is sufficiently congruent with either view to be strongly considered.

Is it necessary to choose between the skeptic's view and the evolutionary-naturalistic perspectives? While there may be some psychological pressure to choose between them, the choice need not be forced if one accepts the idea that they both support the proposed orientation. Perhaps, in addition to the reasons already presented, the bases seem to share an inherent distrust of eternal, unchanging, true values. As a result, holding either perspective makes the choice of one dominant value at the expense of others difficult. However, at some future time a choice may be necessary. For example, there may come a time when our understanding of evolution strongly suggests some other orientation, and at that time a choice will have to be made between the two bases. The strengths and weaknesses of each basis would have to be weighed and debated. At present, however, such a choice does not seem necessary.

One final point should be made before the final chapter. Given the naturalistic-evolutionary perspective, it could be argued that the overriding value orientation should be the promotion of survival or evolution rather than the optimizing orientation. Thus, if survival and freedom should conflict, survival would be valued more. The following points should be considered regarding this issue. First, to argue that survival should be valued over freedom transforms the position from a factual criterion to be employed in choosing a high-level value to a high-level value itself. This constitutes a significant shift in position, and the assertion of value would have to be justified. Second, if the argument in the present chapter is accepted, one need not choose between freedom and survival. On one hand, optimizing alternatives may promote and be necessary for survival. On the other hand, survival seems a clear prerequisite for freedom. Rather than being at odds with one another, freedom and survival may imply one another. Until there is clear and compelling evidence to the contrary, we are not forced to choose either, for the promotion of either may lead to the promotion of both.

Six

A Final Assessment of the Proposed Orientation

Two major persuasive reasons for adopting the optimizing orientation have already been presented: On the one hand, the skeptic's view supports it because the orientation uniquely mitigates the difficulties of unwarranted value imposition. On the other hand, the evolutionary-naturalistic perspective also supports the optimizing orientation because the orientation seems most congruent with the modern understanding of evolution and survival. In addition to these two major reasons, five other reasons may be offered that support the proposed orientation.

Other Reasons for Adoption

1. As suggested earlier, any use of sociological knowledge to change behavior requires manipulation or control. If, contrary to the proposed orientation, this control is used to minimize alternatives in order to either impose or eliminate some valued state, the behavior of the controller may become similarly limited as a result. This apparent paradox occurs because, in trying to insure that only the valued behavior occurs, considerable energy must be directed toward preventing unvalued behavior. The more the actor wishes to behave in ways contrary to the values of the controller, the more surveillance is necessary, and the more assiduously other alternatives must be blocked off. As a result, the behavior of the controller is increasingly dictated and controlled by the target population (even if there is no conscious desire by that population to do so).

2. The growth of the body of sociological knowledge is greatly facilitated by the participation and cooperation of those studied in gaining necessary information. Jourard (1968, p. 3–12) argues that people are increasingly becoming less cooperative with social scientists because they feel that their aid in the knowledge process will not benefit those who are cooperative and will be used to manipulate and control their behavior in ways contrary to their values. If the proposed orientation is adopted and it is seen that the practice of sociology actually increases the alternatives and thus the probability of each person actualizing his *own* values, willingness to participate in the knowledge process will probably increase. Sociology will benefit from members of society feeling that they will benefit by responding to questionnaires honestly, participating in experiments, and permitting access to otherwise privileged information.

3. By accepting support from a society that enables sociologists to pursue sociology as a vocation, the profession incurs an obligation to reciprocate with benefits to society. The pleasure of attaining and appreciating sociological knowledge for itself is not likely to benefit the majority of the population, particularly as that body of knowledge becomes more complex and abstract. However, by contributing to the optimization of freedom sociology satisfies its obligation to benefit society by contributing to the optimization of each member's chances of actualizing his values.

4. It was suggested in Chapter Two that it is extremely difficult to argue that sociological knowledge is valuable for its own sake, since no other nonepistemic value can be invoked which that knowledge would serve to actualize. If freedom is of value, and sociological knowledge is sought and used to enhance the existence of freedom, then that knowledge too is of value. The nonepistemic ethic of the optimization of freedom, then, provides a rationale for holding the value of knowledge. (It should be pointed out that any nonepistemic metavalue, and not only the optimization of freedom, could serve to legitimate sociological knowledge if sociological knowledge contributed to actualizing that metavalue.)

5. Finally, one value that all sociologists probably hold, even those who maintain a value-free position, is freedom of inquiry. This may even be true of any scientist, since the ability of a science to advance knowledge depends upon the ability of a science to define problems for itself and not seek the solution of problems simply because some authority defines them as important (Bendix, 1970, p. 839). This freedom of inquiry, which is valued by and demanded for sociologists, primarily means that the maximum possible number of areas of inquiry be made open. It may quite legitimately be asked how sociologists could justify their demands for optimization of alternatives in areas of prime concern to them while not extending the demand for the optimization of alternatives to others. If sociologists are justified in seeking and maintaining their freedom, presumably freedom should be extended to all others as well, unless sociologists possess some peculiar, unknown characteristics that make them especially worthy of freedom.

We may state this argument more positively. Given that freedom of inquiry is necessary to the growth of sociological knowledge, the proposed ethic should be held because optimizing the freedom of every individual entails the optimization of freedom of inquiry for sociologists.*

---

* While Kelman sees high-level professional values as not being logically derivable from anything else, some of his comments may suggest other persuasive reasons. He outlines several lines of deductive argument, which he does not pursue, but which might be reformulated into additional reasons for adopting the proposed orientation.

First, I can try to show that the desire to choose represents a universal human need, which manifests itself

Before proceeding, it should be reiterated that freedom is a social state, even though it is expressed in terms of individuals. As a result, the optimization of alternatives is an especially appropriate orientation for sociology. Although the alternatives must admittedly be perceived by individuals to be chosen, nevertheless structural and institutional arrangements crucially determine the range of alternatives open to individuals. A wide range of *actual alternatives* must inhere in the social structures of societies if freedom is not merely to be a subjectively felt self-deception. While at some point the extent of existing alternatives must be judged in terms of individuals, the optimization of alternatives is still seen as primarily the result of and embodied in social structures. Since sociology is normally viewed as the discipline that most clearly directs its attention to societal and social structural questions, the proposed orientation seems particularly appropriate to it. While many of the supporting arguments in previous chapters were sufficiently abstract that the optimizing orientation could be considered by any discipline, as long as the orientation is couched in terms of social structural characteristics rather than, say, individual awareness of open alternatives, the orientation has special relevance to sociology.

Three Other Possible Orientations

Any reasonable choice between alternatives involves comparison. This is no less true in choosing an extraepistemic orientation for a profession such as sociology. However, as was pointed out in Chapter Three, even those who are most critical of value-free sociology, and thus most disposed to an extraepistemic orientation, have been more concerned with identifying and justifying value stands that are present in the field than with actually presenting and justifying their own value orientations. While these demands were

---

under different historical circumstances (not only under conditions of oppression).

Second, I can point out that freedom of choice is an inescapable component of other valued states, such as love, creativity, mastery of the environment, or maximization of one's capabilities. Third, I can try to argue that valuing free individual choice is a vital protection against tyranny [1965, p. 35].

argued to have been beneficial in furthering debate, the lack of well presented and justified alternative orientations makes comparison difficult. However, three possible orientations that are implied in the literature may be compared.* Actually, these three orientations are highly interrelated and will undoubtedly be attractive to many sociologists. It is not argued that they are unattractive when held by individual sociologists, but that they are less acceptable than the optimization of freedom as a dominant orientation for the profession as a whole.

Taking Sides. We have argued that the numerous choices made by sociologists should be oriented by a certain state of affairs, namely, societies and social structures that optimize alternatives open to all societal members. The statements of some sociologists suggest that what the discipline should orient itself towards is not a state of affairs, but a particular group or class of people. The question for them is not what we should value, but who. Such an orientation would tell us who we are for and who we are against. In Chapter One, several sociologists were quoted who not only saw value employment in the mainstream of sociology but who also criticized what they saw as a value orientation which supports the side of power elites. As a result, it has been suggested that sociologists switch their allegiances and take the side of the powerless. "Two correctives are needed. One would entail an ideological purification, or reversal: the other would entail change in alliances so that sociologists would not serve elites but other, hitherto dominated groups" (Birnbaum, 1971, p. 734). We are asked to choose sides; Biblarz clearly expresses the available choice: "The alternatives available to sociologists, then, are to continue to serve groups in power, thus using social science for the maintenance and expansion of that power, or to alter their commitment individually and collectively, and begin to use their skills to serve interests of groups without power" (Biblarz, 1969, p. 4).

The question we must ask is on what basis do we choose to

---

* While we have tried to present these orientations clearly, a stronger presentation could best be made by those who advocate them and are willing as a result to develop more detailed and sophisticated arguments. At any rate, possible weaknesses in presentation are not a result of an attempt to make the orientations easier to rule out.

optimize the interests and values of the powerless, or the powerful for that matter, or any class of people at the expense of all others? What characteristic is there in any particular group that makes their interests and values our overriding concern? It was argued in Chapter Three that we must assume that there is no characteristic of individuals or groups that confers special validity on their values. Further, since sociology is ultimately supported and maintained by all of society, an obligation is incurred to benefit all of its members. Thus, it has been proposed that freedom be optimized for every individual, and not only for some chosen group. Admittedly, a particular empirical situation may dictate that in order to bring about a general increase in freedom for all individuals, the freedom of a group of individuals might have to be curtailed, and thus in a specific case one might need to "take sides." However, this in no way implies that we would always take the same sides, or even that we should value taking sides over optimizing freedom for all.

Equality. Another orientation would eliminate inequality, or more positively, seek equality. Freedom and equality are sometimes viewed as values that are at odds with each other. However, this is true only if one takes the view (which was shown earlier to be antithetical to the proposed orientation of optimizing alternatives for every individual) that freedom includes the right to abrogate the freedom of others, repress them, or reduce their alternatives. In fact, not only is equality closely related to any proposed freedom ethic, but a high degree of equality is also necessary for attaining the proposed optimizing society. This is because significant inequality precludes the existence of substantial, meaningful alternatives being open to every individual. The freedom to choose between a Ford and a Cadillac is more illusory than real and presents no alternative of substance if the social structure is arranged so that many cannot even afford a bicycle.

While a high degree of equality is necessary for the optimization of freedom, it is not *sufficient*. All may be equally unfree. Equality in the possession of resources, both social and physical, does not guarantee that those resources have been used to optimize freedom. If equality does not optimize the chances that every individual's values will be actualized, what end does it serve? Further, if there is some other end, why is it of greater value than freedom?

Equality may be viewed as a subgoal to the primary goal of optimizing freedom, and every effort to bring about equality should be evaluated on the basis of whether it in fact leads to a general increase of freedom. Conceived in this way, equality is not sought as a viable ethical alternative to freedom, but because a high degree of equality is a necessary characteristic of a society that optimizes freedom for every individual.

Elimination of Suffering. The final alternative shares features with the preceding two. Gouldner (1968, p. 105) makes explicit why he takes the side of the powerless, or the underdog.

> I have acknowledged a sympathy with the underdog and with impulses to conduct researches from his standpoint. Yet in searching for the justification of my sentiments I must also candidly confess that I see no special virtue in those who are lacking power and authority, just as I see no special virtue that inheres in those who possess power and authority. It seems to me that neither weakness nor power are values that deserve to be prized.
>
> The essential point about the underdog is that he suffers and that his suffering is naked and visible. It is this that makes and should make a compelling demand on us. What makes his standpoint deserving of special consideration, what makes him worthy of sympathy, is that he suffers.

This orientation is extremely difficult to refute because most of us share sympathy for those who suffer. More importantly, it is difficult to reasonably refute because it is based purely on emotion, and we have no logic that enables us to choose between orientations based on this emotional state and those based on others, such as love, hate, or bliss. Yet we may still try to show that this is not the best possible orientation by following the lines of the argument already presented.

First, choosing an orientation that is directed only at one group of sufferers is unwarranted because, as Davis suggests, "most men suffer" (1968, p. 304). Gouldner (1968) also recognizes that others besides the powerless suffer, but his reasons for directing his "sympathy" and "special consideration" primarily toward the powerless seems contradictory: Their suffering is "naked and visible" (p. 105) and "less likely to be known" (p. 106). Regardless of which is the case, it is unclear how the obviousness or the obscurity of one group's suffering makes it especially deserving of our attention and concern.

Even if we state that the avoidable suffering of all men should be eliminated, we still would not have chosen the best possible orientation. Gouldner would probably recognize that what really bothers him is those who suffer *and* did not choose to suffer. If we make the elimination of avoidable suffering our highest value, we would also have to eliminate the suffering of individuals who choose to suffer, such as long distance runners, and those who believe that they must suffer, such as Jesus. This orientation would further eliminate the possibility of choosing to take calculated risks, since they may lead to suffering as well as a substantial good. When suffering is freely and knowingly chosen it is not worthy of our sympathy. What is worthy of our sympathy is when persons have no alternative but to suffer, and we do not seek the knowledge necessary to allow them to avoid suffering. The optimization of alternatives maximizes the possibilities of avoiding suffering, and yet does not prohibit individuals from freely choosing to suffer in order to achieve some more highly valued personal goal.

Influence of a Freedom Orientation on Knowledge

Even if sociologists adopt the optimization of freedom as their nonepistemic orientation, its relationship to what has been recognized as the profession's most basic *epistemic* orientation—an orientation towards truth—is still not specified. Freedom could be given precedence over knowledge, subordinated to it, or shared on an equal status with it. While some may feel it necessary to choose between the first two possibilities, we do not feel so compelled.

Admittedly, in particular situations some sociologists may correctly choose one orientation over the other (for example, in a social situation in which a certain type of knowledge, if sought and obtained by those in power, would most likely be used to decrease alternatives). However, even if such personal choices must be made from time to time, this does not indicate that the profession needs to determine a permanent priority. The adoption of either orientation does not preclude the other; each may be instrumental in actualizing the other's values.

Freedom and "Truth." Three possible lines of reasoning might be offered to show that the adoption of the optimization orientation would lead sociologists away from "truth" and thus preclude attainment of the profession's knowledge goals. These are presented and refuted below.

1. Coherence. One could argue that seeking knowledge according to some values, freedom included, may lead sociology away from truth by removing a coherence or unity which results when the body of knowledge itself solely dictates the search. "Demands for an exclusive priority of social relevance in research and curriculum places a limitation on the consistency and coherence of sociological thought and, therefore, on the development of the discipline. If the choice of problems is guided by extra-disciplinary concerns, and if it is connected to a succession of political and moral issues in society, and if there is acceleration of social change, then research efforts will become fragmented and knowledge will cease to be cumulative" (Silvers, 1969, p. 59).

This criticism would apply to the optimizing orientation only if that orientation entailed the "exclusive priority of social relevance," which as we shall soon see it does not. Also, this criticism assumes that for a body of knowledge to be relevant to an extra-epistemic value, it must be relevant to every fleeting social concern. The proposed orientation is of lasting value. Contrary to the criticism, if the orientation of freedom was adopted by generations of sociologists, it would provide an additional extraepistemic unity and coherence.

2. Objectivity. It may be argued that an orientation of the general optimization of alternatives may preclude truth by preventing sociologists from being objective. Refuting this argument is difficult, since the term *objective* is ambiguous. As Rudner (1966) points out, the term *objective* may be taken as the opposite of *subjective*. In this sense, *subjective* and *objective* mean something similar to "psychological" and "nonpsychological," respectively. This is quite different from *objective* as "unbiased" or "tending to be free from error." "No one has ever demonstrated that psychological, per

se, is identical with the biased; nor is it easy to imagine how a cogent demonstration of this could possibly proceed" (Rudner, 1966, p. 74). Since we would not want to assume that any subjectively determined knowledge is necessarily invalid, *objective* as the opposite of *subjective* is probably not an adequate definition.*

"Dictionary definitions of 'objective' are stated in terms like 'existing independent of the mind,' or 'external to the mind' and so forth" (Taylor, 1968, p. 302). These definitions are also inadequate since, while "truth" may exist outside the mind, our knowledge of it certainly cannot exist *without* a mind. However, we would like our knowledge to correspond closely with the truth, so we might define *objective* as "external to the mind that initially discovers it." This suggests that others could repeat our methods and arrive at the same knowledge—it would allow what Gouldner (1968, p. 113) calls "transpersonal replicability." Herbert Feigel argues for this usage of the term, saying that the fundamental requirement of objectivity of science is "that the knowledge claims of science be in principle capable of the test . . . on the part of any person properly equipped with the intelligence and the technical devices of observation or experimentation" (Vrga, 1971, p. 243).

Thus, objective knowledge is derived from an objective method, which others can repeat, obtaining the same results. However, this transpersonal replicability does not guarantee lack of bias or error. Methods may be highly biased and yet, if they are well explicated, be duplicated with the same erroneous results.

Taylor (1968) circularly concludes that an objective method is one that scientists agree will yield knowledge. This is inadequate because scientists may agree to a highly biased method. More importantly, objective methods must be distinguished from methods that are believed to yield knowledge, since the reason for considering objective methods in the first place is because it helps to determine whether a method is likely to *lead* to knowledge.

Thus, the term *objective* may be too ambiguous to be a very useful concept. However, the concern that holding a value strongly may lead sociology away from truth is significant enough to warrant

---

* Such a definition of *objective* would also rule out the possibility of intersubjective certifiability, which is necessary to many types of research, such as disaster research and participant observation.

a reply. So, for the purpose of this discussion we must use some definition of the term even if it is too crude for philosophers of science. The problem with the previous definitions may be that the most useful referent of objectivity is neither methods nor knowledge, but an *attitude* in selecting methods and seeking knowledge. An attitude of objectivity seeks to eliminate bias wherever possible, and to the maximum degree *allows the empirical world to object* if we misinterpret it. The prime virtue of the value-free position lies not in its conclusion about the ends to which knowledge should be used, but rather in embodying this attitude concerning how knowledge should be sought. The proposed orientation in no way conflicts with this. While valuing the optimization of freedom may dispose us to seek knowledge in some areas rather than others, it does not necessarily lead us to search for alternatives that do not exist or to ignore alternatives that do. Further, there is little reason to think that holding the optimization orientation will negate objectivity, even if one of the previous definitions of the term is employed.*

3. Basic Research. Finally, some may object that if a nonepistemic decision orientation, such as the optimization of alternatives, was strongly held, the value placed on research directly related to the orientation would inhibit pure, or basic, research. In addition, basic research, which is necessary to understanding the workings of society, might not be viewed as relevant. This argument, however, is mistaken in two ways. First, the optimization of alternatives

---

* This is not to say that adopting the optimization orientation would not change the shape of the body of sociological knowledge. Since it would imply a preference for certain areas of inquiry over others, the body of knowledge would undoubtedly differ from what it would be if the orientation had not been chosen. However, this would in no way imply a nonobjective inquiry in these areas or a less satisfactory knowledge of them.

In addition, the proposed orientation may be less biasing than other alternatives, especially those which demand personal involvement with one group to the exclusion of others. Kultgen states:

> The dangers of personal involvement are obvious. They are perhaps the dangers which those who advocate value-free objectivity in science have in mind. Problems of one's group may become more important than the problems of sociology. One's interests, focused in particular loyalties, hopes, and antagonisms, are a source of bias. They dispose one to view evidence selectively and accept arguments which one wants to be true [1970, p. 187].

for every individual entails the optimization of alternatives in sociological inquiry. Thus, the sociological researcher would in no way
be prohibited from doing basic research, but he should make known
the implications of his basic research for freedom as they become
clear.

Second, the process of answering questions that seem directly
applicable to the optimization of freedom may require basic research
that may *not* seem directly applicable. This is often the case when a
social scientist deals with practical problems related to actualizing
valued ends. "A social scientist who undertakes to work on a practical problem . . . quickly finds that the popular or 'common
sense' statement of the problem is either incomplete or misleading:
that 'the problem is really many problems' . . . The social scientist gets driven back to more fundamental questions that bear less
and less resemblance to the practical problem until they appear to
be irrelevant; furthermore, some of these fundamental questions
raised in this way take on a life of their own and become genuinely
dissociated from practical problems" (Beal, 1969, p. 467).

Increased Knowledge and Freedom. Just as a goal of freedom need not work against a goal of knowledge, a goal of knowledge need not work against a goal of freedom. Some might argue
that valuing and seeking knowledge may work against freedom if
the resulting sociological knowledge is used to minimize rather than
optimize alternatives. This could occur. However, it is least likely to
occur when the knowledge orientation is held in conjunction with
the orientation of a general optimization of alternatives. While the
specific means chosen by sociologists to actualize freedom are not
dictated by the orientation, as will be seen in the discussion to follow, making and evaluating the necessary choices with reference to
the freedom orientation is clearly more likely to bring about freedom
than making them on other bases. One choice that is implied by
the optimization of alternatives is that sociologists should attempt
to insure that sociological knowledge is disseminated to the widest
possible public and not confined to the profession or a select few
nonprofessionals, because individuals must be aware of the alternatives that are open to them if they are to take advantage of them in
actualizing their values. This dissemination has not occurred, which
perhaps has been due to an attitude characteristic of all intellectuals

and not just sociologists: "The number of 'intellectuals' has become prodigious. The more the numbers have swelled, the more the members of this category are presumed to have in their keeping possessions of an esoteric nature from which the general public is excluded. Our friends outside the guild, as well as other persons we meet more casually, take it for granted that we have arrived at knowledge that they cannot understand. Gertrude Stein, who used to be charged with unintelligibility, once said that she was writing for herself and strangers. We resemble herself except that we omit the strangers" (Nef, 1962, p. 6).

It should be pointed out in fairness to social scientists that the media have not been very anxious to disseminate social scientific knowledge that would widen the range of general alternatives. Wide dissemination is important for an additional reason. If sociological knowledge is not to be used to control the social structure in order to minimize alternatives open to the public, the public must possess this knowledge in order to be aware of it and to help prevent such control. An analogous case is sociological knowledge used by advertisers to persuade consumers, which becomes increasingly less effective as consumers gain that knowledge. "The increased knowledge benefits not only the persuader but also the target of persuasion. As the persuaders become more sophisticated, so do the people to be persuaded. One way of reading the history of the development of techniques of persuasion is that persuaders have been in a race to keep abreast of the developing resistance of the people to be persuaded" (Bauer, 1968, p. 264).

Nevertheless, wide dissemination of sociological knowledge will not be an easy task. But if competent popularization of sociological knowledge is encouraged, and if recent trends continue toward the publication of mediating periodicals (such as *Society* and *Behavior Today*) and greater mass media interest continue, such dissemination will be possible.

General dissemination of sociological knowledge is just one example of how the union of the orientation of freedom and the orientation of knowledge will increase the likelihood that sociological knowledge will not be used to minimize freedom. More important is the fact that sociological knowledge is necessary to transform social institutions in ways that optimize alternatives open to societal members. In short, the actualization of the optimizing society demands sound, fundamental sociological knowledge.

Thus, the proposed optimization orientation and the profession's current epistemic orientation of truth do not seem to work against each other. Holding either orientation helps to actualize the other and may, in fact, necessitate the holding of the other. As a result, until convincing arguments and evidence to the contrary are presented, sociology is not forced to choose between its epistemic and nonepistemic orientations; rather, it can allow them to operate interdependently and coequally.

Criticisms of the Proposed Orientation

Even if the bulk of the argument to this point is accepted, at least four major criticisms can be leveled against the proposed goal orientation. First, it may be argued that there is no need for a goal orientation to guide decision making in sociology. Second, the proposal may be attacked for seeming to assume that sociologists will act rationally and in accordance with the orientation if they adopt it. Third, the proposed orientation may be criticized for being cast in terms of societal members rather than some other unit. Finally, it may be argued that the proposed orientation needs further specification.

Need for an Orientation. Even if it is accepted that some choice between nonepistemic values is necessary and that the value-free position is neither descriptively nor proscriptively adequate, it might still be argued that no overriding orientation is necessary.

The argument supporting this criticism may be advanced in one of two forms. First, it may be held that what is actually needed is a proper mixture of numerous high-level values (such as cooperation, peace, harmony, beauty, protection from harm, or justice). According to this view, the optimization of alternatives would not be an overriding goal orientation, but just one high-level value to be balanced with numerous others. However, even granting that a large number of high-level values may be chosen by the profession to be actualized, this does not eliminate the need for an overriding highest-level orientation. Once a number of high-level values have been chosen, there are innumerable possible mixes or arrangements of them in relation to one another. A highest-level orientation is needed to determine the most preferable combination. Further, in seeking an acceptable mix, the priorities of some values will conflict, and other values will be incompatible in certain situations. A highest-level orientation is needed to resolve such problems.

Second, some might argue that a basic agreement on the state of affairs that should be sought already exists; the major disagreement centers on the means of actualizing that valued state. As evidence, it might be argued that all major thinkers in all cultures from the earliest times to the present have sought freedom, but have primarily disagreed on the means for obtaining it; thus, the concerns expressed in this work are misplaced. The seeking of freedom has, in fact, been embodied in the works of numerous scholars and in countless actions. However, recognizing this fact does not imply universal support for the optimizing orientation. Clearly, there are also many examples in history of those who have maintained the belief in an innate superiority of their races or groups and thus justified the optimization of alternatives for these people while minimizing alternatives for others. Still others have argued for the accumulation of power, self-interest, or military might at the expense of freedom, often without even offering the misleading rhetoric that the temporary loss of freedom which such goals entail would lead to greater freedom at some later date. The unfortunate fact of the matter is that there are some who fear freedom either for themselves or others. Further, even those who have used the term *freedom* have often intended something clearly different from what was expressed in Chapter Four. For example, calls not to meddle with the free enterprise system made by monopolistic corporate heads clearly involve two conceptions of freedom that were expressly ruled out—freedom from constraints and freedom to abridge the alternatives of others. Also, the three alternative orientations suggested earlier in this chapter could be persuasively argued to be worthwhile candidates for adoption. Presumably, others will also be suggested. In short, while there would hopefully be considerable support for the proposed orientation, there is no reason to assume that it would be universal and that we need only discuss means.

Moreover, valued ends must be generally and explicitly

agreed upon before we can most fruitfully discuss means for their attainment. Finally, while we disagree with the premise underlying this criticism, for the sake of argument let us grant that there is near universal agreement on the proposed orientation. Then the worst this work can be accused of is redundancy; there are no apparent problems, and undoubtedly some benefits, in making this orientation explicit. Further, the discussion has hopefully at least clarified the orientation as well as bases for its choice and justification.

Assumption Concerning Rationality. The orientation may also be attacked for mistakenly assuming that people in general, and sociologists in particular, act rationally. If sociologists adopt this or some other goal orientation, they are expected to act in accord with it. They are expected to refer to the orientation when choosing among types of knowledge to be sought and methods of seeking knowledge, and when evaluating how that knowledge might be used. Doesn't this assume that people will act rationally? In fact doesn't this whole book with its presentation of arguments, consideration of bases for choosing orientations, and hope for future debate imply rationality?

This book does *not* assume that people *are* rational. Many actions seem, to this author, clearly irrational, but at any rate both the concept of rationality and its application to particular instances are extremely hard to analyze. (It often seems that in normal usage "we" are rational and "they" are not.) More positively, we do not wish to deny the importance of nonrational but highly significant creative, emotional, and spiritual sides of human life. Thus, it is by no means assumed that people will act rationally.

However, it is assumed that most people do sincerely try to act rationally and that they believe they are doing so.* That is, people hold high-level values and beliefs and attempt to act in accordance with them, although it is true that personal interests and other factors often cause people to act in ways inconsistent with these values. Although psychological mechanisms may conceal the inconsistency, if the lack of rationality is made clear severe discomfort will be produced. In short, we wish to act in ways that are justifiable to ourselves and as much as possible seem justifiable to

* The author is indebted to Professor John Munkirs who originally suggested this line of reasoning in a conversation.

others. The demands for consistency and rationality vary with individuals and cultures, but generally there is an attempt to act rationally. We may state this assumption differently: At minimum, most people try not to appear irrational either to themselves or to others. If they accept some general principle, they will not knowingly violate it or have others think that they have done so.

Casting the Orientation in Societal Terms. A third general criticism relates to stating the orientation in terms of societies. The choice of societies as a focal unit can be legitimately criticized in at least two ways.

It may be contended that while we sociologists use the term *societies,* usually what we mean, at least implicitly, are *nations.* Similarly, *societal members* may readily be translated to mean *citizens.* It may be more to the point to cast the orientation in terms of nations, since national politics will often be inextricably bound to efforts to expand existing alternatives. Often, however, within the same national boundaries multiple societies may exist, and maintaining the integrity of each society may demand differing social arrangements within a nation. Thus, there are both advantages and disadvantages whether casting the orientation in terms of societies or in terms of nations. *Society* has been used here only because it is so thoroughly infused in the thought of the discipline.

More serious may be the potential criticism that social scientists should have concerns that are directed well beyond their nations. Rather than the narrow focus of optimizing alternatives open to all societal members, we should be concerned with all people; thus, the orientation should be stated in international terms. Whether the orientation should be stated in terms of optimizing alternatives for all people within particular societies or within nations or worldwide is a quandary that the author has not eliminated.

Perhaps selecting this particular goal orientation is due to the fact that the author is a U.S. citizen whose thinking cannot help but be influenced by that fact. Further, it may be that such an orientation is totally inappropriate for sociologists in other societies. In short, it may be that the orientation is in some sense culture-bound, and casting it in international terms may demand the very value imposition it tries to avoid. On the other hand, there seems nothing culture-specific about either of the two alternate bases for the choice of the orientation. Perhaps the only thing that can be done here is to suggest the dilemma in hopes that others might help to resolve it.

Need for Further Specification. Given the need for an overriding orientation, the proposed orientation could be criticized as needing further specification. In some respects this criticism is quite reasonable, and we will address several specific points.

1. No adequate orientation could be so specific as to in essence make all of our decisions for us, and to ask the proposed orientation to do so is clearly unfair. While referring to the orientation should help make many important decisions, it cannot eliminate the continuing need for thought, research, debate, and considered judgment.

2. Although greater specificity in any formulation is generally a virtue, this need not always be the case. If an orientation is to cover wide areas of human affairs and be useful over a considerable period of time, increasing specificity may be too restrictive. Waddington argues in this way, pointing out that while his approach may be charged as being so general that in practice it is useless, the same can be said of any important ethical formulation. Moreover, "No general ethical principle can be useful unless it is wide enough to be relevant to very many diverse aspects of life; and that implies that it cannot be precise enough to obviate the need for debate about particular moral issues" (Waddington, 1960, p. 31).

3. In one special sense, the orientation's lack of specificity may be responsible for its uniqueness and constitutes its prime virtue. It was pointed out earlier that one reason that the term *orientation* was employed rather than the term *ethic* is that the latter, as it is usually employed in philosophy, is more specific and entails a more rule-like or law-like presentation. Since it is truly a general orientation that is sought here, the term *orientation* seems more appropriate and avoids adding ambiguity to the precise meaning of the term *ethic*. Further, an ethic is normally understood to embody a conception of a *substantive* good. At one level, it could be said that the proposed orientation embodies a substantive good, in that societies are valued and sought which optimize alternatives open to societal members. More generally, however, the orientation does not

embody a substantive good—while it calls for more alternatives, it does not specify which choices should be made from this widened selection. It is this lack of specification of a particular substantive good that allows the orientation to simultaneously mitigate the difficulties of unwarranted value imposition and promote evolutionary improvement by not allowing a particular value to dominate the development of the social structure and by keeping alternative courses of development open. In this special sense, the orientation's not specifying a substantive good may be considered its prime virtue. As a result, however, it cannot be applied to many important areas of choice.

4. It may, however, still be legitimately argued that further specification is needed in two important areas. It may be agreed that the means and strategies for actualizing societies that optimize alternatives are important and difficult topics that need discussion. The optimizing orientation could be faulted for not specifying what means should be adopted in actualizing freedom as well as whether to actively bring about changes or merely to monitor the use of knowledge. However, it could be used in evaluating possible means, since some will likely succeed in optimizing freedom, while others would actually minimize it (such as those that falsely request people to "give up these few freedoms in order that your freedom may be protected"). Thus, no overriding goal orientations can dictate the particular means but they can guide the choice.* For example, Kelman (1965) suggests some means implied by an orientation toward freedom of choice (see Table 1). These might not be considered the best possible approaches the sociologist might take in actualizing the optimization of freedom orientation, because they do not involve enough active participation in bringing about fundamental changes in social structures. While this orientation does not dictate means, thus leaving them open to debate, it helps in making choices by acting as a referent for the debate.

5. Finally, some feel that the orientation needs to specify the ultimate state of affairs being sought, that is, the specific social situations, structures, and systems. While the orientation does not itself

---

* Sociologists have often told the public: "If you tell me your values, I will tell you what they imply and how to actualize them." Presumably they are capable of doing the same for sociologists.

TABLE 1. Means for Actualizing the Maximization of
Alternatives Orientation.

Desirable Steps	Role of Practitioner	Role of Applied Researcher	Role of Basic Researcher
Increasing awareness of manipulation	Labeling own values to self and clients; allowing clients to give feedback	Evaluating organization that will use findings; considering on whom, how, and in what context they will be used	Predicting probabilities of different uses of research product given existing socio-historical context
Building protection against or resistance to manipulation into the social science process	Minimizing own values and maximizing clients' values as dominant criteria for change	Helping target group to protect its interests and resist encroachments on its freedom	Studying processes of resistance to control; communicating findings to the public
Setting enhancement of freedom of choice as a positive goal	Using professional skills and relationship to increase clients' range of choices and ability to choose	Promoting opportunities for increased choice on part of target group	Studying conditions for enhancement of freedom of choice and maximization of individual values

Source: Adapted from Kelman (1965, p. 41).

delineate these, it does help in choosing among possibilities. The optimization of freedom, for example, may suggest that a society revise laws dealing with victimless crimes, open alternatives for minorities, or reallocate resources. On a global level, it suggests that the population should be reduced to increase alternatives and that individuals be allowed to move freely between social systems. While a lasting orientation can guide the choices of valued states for each generation, it cannot dictate which states will permanently optimize alternatives. The optimum possible range of alternatives depends both on our knowledge of the current range and on the predictions arising from current knowledge of how various manipulations of the social structure will influence that range. Thus, our specific choices would depend not only on the orientation, but also on the changing state of the body of knowledge. Even if the proposed orientation is accepted, these specific choices will undoubtedly be the subject of difficult debate, research, and interpretation.

General features of the optimizing society also demand attention and debate, such as the areas of priority in widening alternatives. One particular feature of the optimizing society that needs specifying is what might be termed the *system of distribution,* that is, how to optimize alternatives for every individual rather than just a popular majority or an elite. However, this raises important issues about the distribution of rights, duties, and advantages. This constitutes an area in which research must be done by those who adopt the proposed orientation.

Especially useful to the consideration of this question is a recent work, *A Theory of Justice* by Rawls (1971)'. While it is beyond the scope of this work to adequately consider the insights of Rawls and his critics, Rawls's work suggests types of thinking that may be fruitfully explored, and it seems highly consistent with the main thrust of the proposed optimization orientation. He recognizes that at an institutional level, the most just system may also demand a certain amount of inequality. For him, a system consists of two principles: The first principle deals with the distribution of rights and obligations, while the second deals with the distribution of advantages. "First: each person is to have an equal right to the most extensive basic liberty comparable with a similar liberty for others. Second: social and economic inequalities are to be arranged so that they are both (a) reasonably expected to be to everyone's advantage, and (b) attached to positions and offices open to all" (Rawls, 1971, p. 60). Thus Rawls recognizes that any distributive systems must probably have within them inequalities, but these must be justified by their leading to advantages that the least advantaged in society would not accrue otherwise. (For an excellent review of *A Theory of Justice,* see Hampshire, 1972.)

6. No proposed orientation is likely to be sufficiently specific for all. But it is argued here that some basic agreement on orientation is necessary before settling on a specific form. Further, after adoption, any orientation will continually be revised and reformulated. The profession of medicine is clearly oriented toward health, and yet what constitutes health and the means to achieve and main-

tain it are always being revised. As useful as the general orientation of justice is to the legal profession, its exact nature is under constant debate and refinement, and the necessary basic orientation toward justice does not specify what is just in a particular case. Similarly, sociology's epistemic orientation is similarly general and its exact nature and the means to best utilize it are subject to debate. We are not trying to minimize the difficulties in carrying such a debate to a conclusion; we are only suggesting that the choice of an orientation precedes it. While the freedom orientation suffers from the same lack of specificity as do other ethics, it does make possible the lower-level value choices, and thus represents a gain in specificity over previous positions. Further, adopting this orientation will provide answers to many questions that have been central to the value debate.

We need no longer ask what we value—we can explicitly state that we value the optimization of alternatives for every individual. When we are asked "Knowledge for what?", we may reply, "Freedom." This same freedom has now been specified as the "ultimate benefit" to which sociology is directed.

We assume that the debate over the role and nature of values within sociology is valuable and is likely to continue. This work does not presume to end the debate, but rather to further it by clarifying current positions as well as suggesting both a new position and bases for positions which might serve as new foci for further debate. The value-free and related positions are neither descriptively nor prescriptively useful. Although recent counterpositions have performed a valuable service in pointing out weaknesses in the value-free stance and showing the need for an extraepistemic orientation, they have not suggested the nature of, or offered bases for, the choice of a new orientation that would provide a goal for the discipline, orienting the numerous decisions that must be made and that demand reference to values in addition to expanding our knowledge. Two possible bases for choosing an orientation have been examined—the skeptic's view and the naturalistic-evolutionary view. Both views, while critical of one another and representing fundamentally divergent world views, suggest and support an orientation that demands the search for social structures which optimize alternatives open to societal members.

We may now turn to the question of alternatives for one final time. The most basic alternatives open to the profession are to choose an orientation that optimizes alternatives or one that maximizes some other value and abridges the societal members' right to choose. Similarly, we must choose whether to promote a wider number of alternatives and thus open new paths of development or to allow possible courses of development to be closed by perfecting social structures according to some particular value. The most basic choice facing sociology, then, is to widen objectively existent areas of choice, or to minimize them.

Value:
Uses of the Term

In Chapter One it was pointed out that, consistent with traditional usage, the following working definition of the term *value* was chosen: "beliefs about classes of objects, situations, actions, and wholes composed of them in regards to the extent that they are good, right, obligatory, or ought to be." While there may be general agreement on the usage of the term, there is considerable disagreement as to how some of the key words of the definition, such as "good" and "obligatory," are themselves to be defined, as well as major disagreements about theories of value and their justifications. Further, there is some controversy on distinctions and qualifications that should be made in the use of the term. Since some distinctions clarify our thinking about the term, and because discussion of them will clarify the way the term is used in this book, we will discuss

112

them briefly in this appendix. At the outset it should be pointed out that this working definition conceives of value rather broadly, gathering together several distinguishable judgments of value.

Most social scientists and, surprisingly, large numbers of philosophers use the term *value* to refer to beliefs about what is good on one hand and what is obligatory on the other. However, these two uses are distinguishable. Although such a distinction may not be necessary for some types of general discussion, we will consider subcategories of the term *value judgments*, as do such philosophers as Frankena (1973).* Thus, we distinguish *judgments of obligation* from *judgments of value*. Judgments of obligation refer to actions which we consider right, wrong, or obligatory. A judgment of value (with *value* used in a more specific sense) refers not to actions but to persons, objects, states of affairs, motivations, characteristics, and so on. We may consider them to be good, bad, virtuous, blameworthy, despicable, and so forth (Frankena, 1973, p. 9).

Further, within judgments of value we may distinguish judgments of *moral* and *nonmoral* value. Frankena (1973, pp. 9–10) points out that judgments of moral value refer to persons, motives, intentions, character traits, and the like. Examples are: "My father is a good man"; "Jones's character is admirable"; "Benevolence is a virtue"; and "Jealousy is an ignoble motive." Judgments of nonmoral value apply not to persons or motives, but "all sorts of other things such as cars, paintings, experiences, forms of government, and what not. We say they are good, bad, desirable, undesirable, and so on, but we do not mean that they are morally good or bad, since they are generally not the kinds of things that can be morally good or bad" (Frankena, 1973, pp. 9–10). Examples are: "That is a good car"; "Miniver Cheevy did not have a very good life"; "Pleasure is a good in itself"; and "Democracy is the best form of government."

Since discussions of ethics usually deal with moral obligation, we may similarly distinguish moral from nonmoral obligation, even though both refer to actions. Examples of judgments of moral

---

* Indeed this part of the discussion is heavily indebted to the insightful analysis provided by Frankena (1973). The examples given in the following discussion of types of value judgments are either taken directly from or closely follow Frankena.

obligation are: "We ought to keep our promises"; "I ought to be charitable"; "We have an obligation to fight for our country"; and "All men have a right to rebel when oppressed." Nonmoral judgments of obligation, while important to the practical aspects of everyday life, are not usually considered in ethical discourse. Frankena (1973, p. 11) offers the following examples of nonmoral judgments of obligation: "You ought to buy a new suit"; "You just have to go to that concert"; "In building a bookcase one should use nails, not Scotch tape"; and "The right thing to do on fourth down with thirteen yards to go is to punt."

These distinctions are not crucial to all forms of discourse dealing with values, as, for example, in discussions of whether values have any place at all within a discipline. However, the distinctions are often very valuable, both because the different types of value judgments often demand different sorts of justifications, and because there may be different types of relationships between them.

For example, judgments of moral and nonmoral obligation demand different sorts of justification. Justifications for a judgment of nonmoral obligation, such as "Members of the army ought to keep their rifles clean and in good repair," are considerably different from justifications for a judgment of moral obligation, such as "One ought to join the army if one's country is threatened." Further, differences in positions may often hinge on explicit or implicit differences on the relations between the types of value judgments. For example, two persons may both judge just societies to be good, but they may strongly differ as to what actions, if any, they are obligated to perform as a result of this judgment. One may claim, "Since I value a just society, I am obligated to do that which brings it about. In short, I ought to do all in my power to make this society more just." The other, however, may hold, "I am by no means obligated to help attain such a society. While I may approve of your attempting to bring about a just society, my valuing such a society incurs no personal obligation." What both parties are disagreeing about is the relation between judgments of value and judgments of obligation. Not distinguishing between types of judgments often means that the nature of the disagreement is not pinpointed, and the discussion cannot be shifted to a more fruitful level.

This book deals primarily with questions of actions of individual sociologists and of the discipline as a whole, and as such its primary concern is with judgments of obligation. Since the present author personally feels uncomfortable with such terms as *obligation* and *duty*, and since arguments in the social science literature are seldom argued in such a strong fashion, these concepts do not appear here; the discussion centers around what we as a profession and as individuals ought or ought not to do. Thus, the types of questions that are addressed are: Ought sociologists to seek knowledge purely for its own sake or ought they to use it in actualizing other value ends? How should knowledge be disseminated? Ought sociologists to work for a particular group within society as opposed to others or the society as a whole? Ought sociologists to act to change societies in certain directions? The ultimate concern of this work, then, is to consider what sort of value orientation should guide the practicing sociologist and the discipline in choosing future courses of action and evaluating past actions.

While the various positions that are discussed focus on judgments of obligation, considerable attention is devoted to judgments of value made by each position. This is because while on many levels there is considerable disagreement between the various positions, they share an implicit teleological theory of obligation, which sees judgments of obligation as intimately linked to judgments of value. They are teleological in that judgments about whether an act ought to be carried out are based upon the probable *future consequences*. More specifically, teleological theories hold that we ought to do those things which are likely to lead to valued states of affairs. Thus, judgments of obligation demand discussion of judgments of value if one holds a teleological theory. Teleological theories of obligation can perhaps be understood more clearly by contrasting them to deontological theories of obligation, which argue that what ought to be done does not depend on the good produced by an act; rather, there are characteristics of certain acts *themselves* that make them obligatory regardless of their consequences. Thus, a deontological view might be that one ought to keep promises because it is inherently just or because it is commanded by God, and not because it would lead to some valued consequences. (For a more extended discussion of teleological and deontological theories of obligation, see Frankena, 1973, pp. 14–33.) The thing to bear in mind is that the various positions discussed in this work, while differing at many levels, share an implicit teleological theory of obligation.

There are a few additional distinctions and qualifications concerning the term *value* that should be made. First, while the term is used here as a noun, it also has verb forms. Terms such as *valuing* are used to suggest an active process, such as the act of comparison, rather than a more passive notion of the results of the process. Some, in fact, would prefer the verb form since it inhibits viewing values as unchanging or eternal. While this perspective should be kept in mind, it also seems that we can discuss at any point in the continuous valuing process its products; as a result the noun usage, in addition to being the predominant convention, also has some merit. At any rate, those who usually employ the verb form use it in ways consistent with the working definition. "For Dewey and Richard M. Hare it [valuation] covers judgments about what is right, wrong, obligatory, or just, as well as judgments about what is good, bad, desirable, or worthwhile" (Frankena, 1967, p. 230).

Dewey (1939) also distinguishes two types of valuing—mere desiring or liking (described by such terms as *to prize, to esteem, to hold dear,* or *to like*) and involving active reflection and comparison (described by such terms as *to appraise, to evaluate,* or *to valuate*). The working definition is in line with this second usage. Although in common parlance we often use the term to refer to personal preferences, as in "I value chocolate over vanilla ice cream," the term here is used to refer to judgments of a higher-level value with significant social implications. Thus, we distinguish between personal preference and value judgments (although value judgments may influence personal preference), and recognize values (as does Lewis, 1969, pp. 3–5), even in discussions of individual ethics, in relation to human groups, societies, and humanity generally. Sociologists have, of course, been quick to recognize values as primarily social, even though they may be internalized by individuals. Philosophers also recognize this, as this comment on morality by Frankena (1973, p. 6) indicates: "Now, morality in the sense indicated is, in one aspect at least, a social enterprise, not just a discovery or invention of the individual for his own guidance. Like one's language, state, or church, it exists before the individual, who is inducted into it and becomes more or less of a participant in it, and it goes on existing after him. Moreover, it is not social merely in the sense of being a system governing the relations of one individual to others, . . . it is also largely social in its origins, sanctions, and functions."

The distinction between *value* as used here in its important social sense and as an expression of personal preferences can perhaps be most clearly realized when we recognize that the two often conflict. Individually, we often possess strongly held personal preferences for certain acts. It is often precisely the group and societal level values which we have internalized that prevent us from acting upon our preferences. Similarly, the possession of values often compels us to act in ways that would not occur if the matter were one of simple personal preference.

Further, since both are beliefs that are preeminently social even when internalized by individuals, it is also well to distinguish between attitudes and values. Rokeach (1968, pp. 159–160) argues that an attitude may be conceptualized as "an organization of several beliefs focused on a specific object (physical or social, concrete or abstract) or situation." A value, on the other hand, is a "belief that a specific mode of conduct or end-state of existence is preferable to alternative modes of conduct or end-states of existence. Once a value is internalized it becomes, consciously or unconsciously, a standard or criterion for guiding action, for developing and maintaining attitudes toward relevant objects and situations, for morally judging self and others, and for comparing self with others" (p. 160). Rokeach points out that his definition is consistent with those of Clyde Kluckhohn, Brewster Smith, and Robin Williams, and that value, once so defined, differs considerably from attitude. "While an attitude represents several beliefs focused on a specific object or situation, a value is a single belief that transcendentally guides actions and judgments across specific objects and situations, and beyond immediate goals to more ultimate end-states of existence. Moreover, a value, unlike an attitude, is an imperative to action, not only a belief about the preferable but also a preference for the preferable. Finally, a value, unlike an attitude, is a standard or yardstick to guide actions, attitudes, comparisons, evaluations, and justifications of self and others" (Rokeach, 1968, p. 160).

One final point should be made. While we concur with

Rokeach that attitudes represent several beliefs and values single beliefs, we (and undoubtedly Rokeach as well) do not imply that values occur in isolation. Our understanding of groups and societies suggests that single values do not exist in isolation but rather occur within total systems. That is, the values within the system tend to be interrelated and often within the system there are sets of values that are mutually supportive. This is not to say that values within a system never conflict or that there are no internal contradictions, but that single values may be placed in the context of the whole of which they are parts. The difficulty is that while we sometimes discuss total value systems, it is often necessary to consider value judgments separately, either because we lack the capacity to consider them all at once or we consider the probable lack of clarity in doing so imprudent. The point is that even when a value is considered apart from the total system, it is well to recognize that changes in it will likely have implications for other values as well.

In summary, a broad definition of the term *value,* consistent with the usages of philosophers and social scientists, is "beliefs about classes of objects, situations, actions, and wholes composed of them, . . . in regards to the extent that they are good, right, obligatory, or ought to be." Within the broad working definition, several distinguishable categories of value judgments are lumped together. Following Frankena (1973), judgments of value are distinguished from judgments of obligation, and within each category moral and nonmoral subcategories are distinguished. Since this work primarily concerns actions of individual sociologists and of the profession as a whole, it primarily focuses on questions of what ought to be done, or questions of obligation. However, since the positions that are discussed implicitly hold to a teleological theory of obligation that sees the way we ought to act as tied to the value of the probable consequences of an act, judgments of value are given considerable attention. Further, the use of the noun form is justified; values are differentiated from personal preferences, with their social nature stressed, and from attitudes; and values occur within systems rather than in isolation.

References

ABELSON, P. H. "Social Responsibilities of Scientists." *Science,* 1970, *167,* 241.

ACTON, H. B. "Georg Wilhelm Freidrich Hegel." In P. Edwards (Ed.), *The Encyclopedia of Philosophy.* Vol. 3–4. New York: Macmillan, 1967.

ADAMS, E. M. *Ethical Naturalism and the Modern World View.* Chapel Hill: University of North Carolina Press, 1960.

ANDREW, G. "Some Observations on Management Problems in Applied Social Research." *American Sociologist,* 1967, *2,* 89.

BAUER, R. A. " 'Social Responsibility' or Ego Enhancement?" *Journal of Social Issues,* 1965, *21,* 47–54.

BAUER, R. A. "Limits of Persuasion." In H. H. Martin and K. E. Anderson (Eds.), *Speech Communication.* Boston: Allyn & Bacon, 1968.

BEAL, G. M. "Some Issues We Face." *Rural Sociology,* 1969, *34,* 461–475.

119

BECKER, H. S. "Whose Side Are We On?" *Social Problems,* 1967, *14,* 239–247.

BELL, D. "The Social Science Press: The United States of America." *International Social Science Journal,* 1967, *19*(2), 245–254.

BENDIX, R. "Sociology and the Distrust of Reason." *American Sociological Review,* 1970, *35,* 831–843.

BENNE, K. D. "The Responsible Behavioral Scientist: An Introduction." *Journal of Social Issues,* 1965, *21,* 1–8.

BENNIS, W. C. "Future of the Social Sciences." *Antioch Review,* 1968, *28,* 227–255.

BIBLARZ, A. "On the Question of Objectivity in Sociology." *et al.,* 1969, *2,* 2–5.

BIERSTEDT, R. "Social Science and Social Policy." *American Association of University Professors Bulletin,* 1948, *34,* 310–319.

BIRNBAUM, N. "Sociology: Discontent Present and Perennial." *Social Research,* 1971, *38,* 732–750.

BOULDING, K. E. "Dare We Take the Social Sciences Seriously?" *American Behavioral Scientist,* 1967, *10,* 12–16.

BRANDT, R. B. *Ethical Theory.* Englewood Cliffs, N.J.: Prentice-Hall, 1959.

BRAUDE, L. "Ethical Neutrality and the Perspective of the Sociologist." *Sociological Quarterly,* 1964, *5,* 396–399.

CARO, F. G. "Approaches to Evaluation Research: A Review." *Human Organization,* 1969, *28,* 87–99.

COHN-BENDIT, D., and others. "Why Sociologists?" *Partisan Review,* 1968, *35,* 543–549.

COLFAX, J. D. "Knowledge for Whom? Relevance and Responsibility in Sociological Research." *Sociological Inquiry,* 1970, *40,* 73–83.

COSER, L. A. "Social Involvement or Scientific Detachment—The Sociologist's Dilemma." *Antioch Review,* 1968, *28,* 108–113.

COSER, L. A. "Letter to a Young Sociologist." *Sociological Inquiry,* 1969, *39,* 131–138.

DAVIS, A. E. "About Truth, Objectivity, and Values." *American Sociologist,* 1968, *3,* 303–304.

DEWEY, J. *Theory of Valuation.* Chicago: University of Chicago Press, 1939.

DEWEY, R., and HUMBER, W. S. *An Introduction to Social Psychology.* Part IV. New York: Macmillan, 1966.

DOBZHANSKY, T. *The Biological Basis of Human Freedom.* New York: Columbia University Press, 1956.

DORN, D. S., and LONG, G. L. "Brief Remarks on the Association's Code of Ethics." *American Sociologist,* 1974, *9,* 31–35.

EISELE, V. "Theory and Praxis: The View from Frankfort." *Berkeley Journal of Sociology,* 1971–1972, *16,* 94–105.

ETZKOWITZ, H. "Toward a Radical Restructuring of Society." *et al.,* 1969, *2,* 12.

EULAU, H. "Values in Behavioral Science: Neutrality Revisited." *Antioch Review,* 1968, *28,* 160–167.

FRANKENA, W. K. "Values and Valuation." In P. Edwards (Ed.), *The Encyclopedia of Philosophy.* Vol. 7–8. New York: Macmillan, 1967.

FRANKENA, W. K. *Ethics.* Englewood Cliffs, N.J.: Prentice-Hall, 1973.

GOULDNER, A. W. "Anti-Minotaur: The Myth of a Value-Free Sociology." *Social Problems,* 1962, *9,* 199–213.

GOULDNER, A. W. "The Sociologist as Partisan: Sociology and the Welfare State." *American Sociologist,* 1968, *3,* 103–116.

GRAY, D. J. "Value-Free Sociology: A Doctrine of Hypocrisy and Irresponsibility." *Sociological Quarterly,* 1968, *9,* 176–185.

HAMPSHIRE, S. "A Special Supplement: A New Philosophy of the Just Society." *New York Review of Books,* February 24, 1972, pp. 34–39.

HANCOCK, R. N. *Twentieth Century Ethics.* New York: Columbia University Press, 1974.

HAUSER, P. H. "On Actionism in the Craft of Sociology." *Sociological Inquiry,* 1969, *39,* 139–147.

HOROWITZ, I. L. *Ideology and Utopia in the United States 1956–1976.* New York: Oxford University Press, 1977.

JENSEN, A. R. "How Much Can We Boost IQ and Scholastic Achievement?" *Harvard Educational Review,* 1969, *39,* 1–123.

JOURARD, S. M. *Disclosing Man to Himself.* New York: D. Van Nostrand, 1968.

KAPLAN, A. *The Conduct of Inquiry.* San Francisco: Chandler, 1964.

KELMAN, H. C. "Manipulation of Human Behavior: An Ethical Dilemma for the Social Scientist." *Journal of Social Issues,* 1965, *21,* 31–46.

KRASNER, L. "The Behavioral Scientist and Social Responsibility: No Place to Hide." *Journal of Social Issues,* 1965, *21,* 9–30.

KULTGEN, J. H. "The Value of Value Judgments in Sociology." *Sociological Quarterly,* 1970, *11,* 181–193.

LAZARSFELD, P. F., SEWELL, W. H., and WILENSKY, H. L. (Eds.). *The Uses of Sociology.* New York: Basic Books, 1967.

LEWIS, C. I. *Values and Imperatives: Studies in Ethics* (J. Lange, Ed.). Palo Alto, Calif.: Stanford University Press, 1969.

LUNDBERG, G. A. *Can Science Save Us?* London: Longman, 1947.

LYND, R. S. *Knowledge for What?* Princeton, N.J.: Princeton University Press, 1948.

MERTON, R. K. "Basic Research and Potentials of Relevance." *American Behavioral Scientist,* 1963, *6,* 86–90.

MOORE, G. E. *Principia Ethica.* Cambridge, England: University Press, 1903.

MULLER, H. J. *Science and Criticism.* New Haven, Conn.: Yale University Press, 1964.

NAGEL, E. *The Structure of Science: Problems in the Logic of Scientific Explanation.* New York: Harcourt Brace Jovanovich, 1961.

NEF, J. "Is the Intellectual Life an End in Itself?" *Review of Politics,* 1962, *24,* 3–18.

PACKARD, V. O. *The Hidden Persuaders.* New York: McKay, 1957.

PERRY, R. B. *Realms of Value.* Cambridge, Mass.: Harvard University Press, 1954.

PHILLIPS, D. L. *Knowledge from What?: Theories and Methods in Social Research.* Chicago: Rand McNally, 1971.

RAWLS, J. *A Theory of Justice.* Cambridge, Mass.: Belknap, 1971.

ROKEACH, M. *Beliefs, Attitudes, and Values: A Theory of Organization and Change.* San Francisco: Jossey-Bass, 1968.

RUDNER, R. S. *Philosophy of Social Science.* Englewood Cliffs, N.J.: Prentice-Hall, 1966.

SHOSTAK, A. B. (Ed.). *Putting Sociology to Work.* New York: McKay, 1974.

SILVERS, R. J. "In Defense of Socially Irrelevant, Scientifically Significant Research." *Canadian Review of Sociology and Anthropology,* 1969, *6,* 58–61.

STOUFFER, S. A. *The American Soldier.* Princeton, N.J.: Princeton University Press, 1949.

TARTER, D. E. "Heeding Skinner's Call: Toward the Development of a Social Technology." *American Sociologist,* 1973, *8,* 153–158.

TAYLOR, K. W. "Rules of Evidence." *American Sociologist,* 1968, *3,* 301–303.

VRGA, D. J. "Social Function of Social Scientists in the Scientific and Atomic Age." *Sociologia Internationalis,* 1971, *9*(2), 240–247.

WADDINGTON, C. H. *The Ethical Animal.* New York: Atheneum, 1960.

WEBER, M. "Science as a Vocation." In H. H. Gerth and C. Wright Mills (Eds.), *From Max Weber: Essays in Sociology.* New York: Oxford University Press, 1946.

WOLFF, K. H. *The Sociology of Georg Simmel.* New York: Free Press, 1950.

Index

The Value Controversy in Sociology

This new book focuses on the current debate over values in sociology and questions which goals are truly appropriate for the discipline. Dennis Foss describes existing positions and argues these positions as strongly as possible. Particular emphasis is given to *value freedom,* which has dominated the field and which suggests that sociologists remain neutral with respect to all values and seek knowledge for its own sake. By critically examining this and other views, Foss proposes that the debate be carried to a different level and that a "decision or goal orientation" serve as a new focal point for the sociological controversy.

Two opposing views are considered as bases for this new orientation. The *skeptic's view* holds that there is a radical split between facts and values, with values ultimately being unsupportable. The *naturalistic-evolutionary view* maintains that values and facts are interconnected and that the choice of values depends on how these values contribute to evolution and survival. Foss argues that both views suggest an *optimizing orientation*—one where decisions about seeking and using knowledge are guided by